You are a theologian. When we come to worship, we are assuming certain things about God and his works. So, is our worship in line with the truths that God teaches us about who he is and what he has accomplished? Along with her theological depth, Amy Gannett's knack at clear and beautiful prose puts this exploration at the top of any good reading list! Read, mark, and inwardly digest this book and you'll never go to church the same way.

Michael Horton, professor of theology,
Westminster Seminary California

Amy Gannett's new book *Fix Your Eyes: How Our Study of God Shapes Our Worship of Him* faithfully reminds us that our knowledge of God awakens a greater love for God, which fuels our worship of God. In a world that is often looking for a mystical feeling or an experience of God, Amy warmly and winsomely invites us to think deeply in our quest to know God more intimately. If you've ever felt intimidated by the study of theology, this book is a needed and welcome resource to add to your library.

Melissa Kruger, author and director of Women's
Initiatives for The Gospel Coalition

FIX
YOUR
EYES

AMY GANNETT

FIX
YOUR
EYES

HOW OUR STUDY
OF GOD SHAPES OUR
WORSHIP OF HIM

BHPUBLISHING.COM

To my dad—

For cultivating my love for theology
over endless cups of coffee on the deck.

Acknowledgments

I signed the contract to write this book less than forty-eight hours after Austin and I brought our first child, Emerson, home from the hospital. That was March 2020, a year that would prove unpredictable, at its best; deafeningly difficult at its worst. As a blumbering new mom and new church planter bent on surviving 2020, it would only be suitable if this section of thanks was as long as the book itself.

Thank you to the exceptional team at B&H—especially to Ashley Gorman for being a keen editor and for championing this message from beginning to end. There's a certain joy that comes when your publishing partners, from editors to marketing team, can (and will) enthusiastically nerd-out about theology with you. This joy has been gratefully mine.

Thank you to my agent and friend, Austin Wilson, who sat in that first theology class with me at Moody Bible Institute all those years ago, and who helped this project become all that the Lord had for it to be.

There are not words of gratitude sufficient for my local prayer team. Tiffany Shepard, Susan McKnight, Dr. Joan Perry, and Anne Albritton: the Lord heard your prayers. He buoyed me up for the work of writing after sleepless nights with a newborn and granted me eagerness to see these truths distilled for the everyday believer. Thank you; you are my partners in the gospel. (Joan, you told pre-baby me that newborns sleep a lot. For this I forgive you.)

To the leaders at Grace Fellowship Church (our sending church) and Trinity Church Greenville (our church plant)—thank you for enthusiastically granting me the space and attention for this work. Thank you, even more, for seeing it as a part of my ministry labor in the local church, and for being the community in which these truths find their feet in my own life.

Gospel-driven parents are a gift, and mine are an embarrassment of riches. Mom and Dad, you were the first to identify and nurture my love for theology. Thank you for giving me weird birthday gifts like books on dispensational theology, and for never backing down from a theological debate. Dad—a family friend once told me that you always wanted a son who shared your love for theology, but God gave you me and you never once considered it a diminished gift. Thank you. I feel that in my bones. Mom—you're a theological powerhouse and the best editor a girl could ask for. To my in-laws, Glenn and Karla, and sister-in-law, Kamille, for their prayers and hours of childcare, I could not be more grateful.

To Emerson—who is the brightest spot in my day and the joy of my heart—for sharing me with this work, I am grateful. My most constant prayer is that you will one day know and love God who has upended my life with rescue and delight.

And finally to Austin—my husband, my friend, my co-church planter, my partner in the gospel—thank you for believing in this work, verbally processing with me when it was highly inconvenient, and for piling my desk high with the best theological resources. Thank you for the way you've passed the gospel back and forth between us. You are God's truest picture of the gospel to me each day.

Glory to the Word of God made flesh who gives our little, meager words meaning and substance—and who will one day see them through to redemption.

Contents

The Necessary Marriage of Theology and Worship

> As I often tell my students, theology is for doxology
> and devotion—that is, the praise of God and the
> practice of godliness. . . . Theology is at its healthiest
> when it is consciously under the eye of the God of
> whom it speaks, and when it is singing to his glory.[1]
>
> *J. I. Packer*

Y ou are a theologian," he spoke calmly into the silent classroom.

Something about the thin, round glasses hanging on the end of the professor's nose and the bow tie neatly tucked beneath his white collar made him feel all the more believable, and made my eyes widen in surprise.

It was my first day of Bible school, and I was sitting in my very first class. While freshman year held a host of uncomfortable, nervous, and intimidating moments, this one will always be etched in my mind. His voice reverberated with age, experience,

---

[1] J. I. Packer, *Concise Theology: A Guide to Historic Christian Beliefs* (Carol Stream, IL: Tyndale House Publishers, 2001), xii.

and authority, and his words struck my timid heart with surprise and self-doubt.

"*You* are a theologian," he repeated.

I gulped. At just nineteen years old, I could name several theologians (most of them dead), and the fact that I could name them made me actually quite proud. Unlike my peers in my high school youth group, I had developed a young knack for reading theological texts. I spent my weekends immersed in systematic theologies, books on the end times, and C. S. Lewis classics. (I was so cool, I know.) I could name famous theologians throughout history and theologians alive today, but my own name never made the list.

After letting us shift nervously in our seats for a few moments, my professor went on to explain what he meant. He told us that theology, for all the complexities we assign it, has a rather simple definition: the study of God. Or, put even more plainly, *theology is what we know and believe about God.*

And, he insisted, that meant something significant for us. It meant that even we—dweeby little eighteen- and nineteen-year-olds—were theologians. We had beliefs about God, and those very beliefs were the content of our theology. Whether we had picked up on subtle teaching over the years past or studied doctrine intentionally, each of us had a theology, which meant that before we had taken a single class, sat for a single exam, written a single paper, or even enrolled in Bible school, each of us was a theologian.

"You already are a theologian," he continued to insist, ". . . but are you a good one?"

My professor's words hung in the air like the sticky humidity of that Midwestern September day. My stomach dropped, my mouth went dry, the intended results of his words taking full form. I had never considered myself a theologian. In fact, I was in that very classroom, enrolled in that very Theology 101 class in order to *become* a theologian. I wanted to learn from the "professional" Christians, dedicating four years of my young life to studying theology in hopes that I might incrementally grow into someone who could maybe, possibly, *someday* consider myself a theologian.

And yet there I was: precisely six minutes into my academic career, being told that I had been a theologian all along, and suddenly questioning the quality of what I truly believed.

Now, maybe you've never set foot in a seminary classroom. Maybe it's on your bucket list or maybe the very idea intimidates you. Maybe you are reading this because you're already "into" theology and you like reading books about it. Or, maybe you are reading this because you're wondering if you *could* be into theology, and this is your first attempt to dip your toe in its waters. Regardless of where you sit on this particular day—a wheeled work chair at a corporation, a rocking chair in a nursery, a plastic seat in a classroom, a friend's sofa you're crashing on for a bit while you figure out your next step in life—there's something you and I have in common: we have some set of beliefs when it comes to God. And those beliefs matter. They matter because they form and inform a thousand tiny decisions we make every day, and because they underline one great big reality in our lives: what we make of God.

Allow me to (gently) pass along to you the same gut-punch my professor gave me on my first day of classes: you're not here to become a theologian. You, my friend, already are one.

Before you picked up this book or any other, you have a view of God. You have a theology tucked inside your bones. If it's anything like mine, you've picked it up along the course of life in a million different places, both aware and unaware. And because theology is what we believe about the God of the universe, the stakes are high. It's imperative that we take an intentional look at our theology and ask: Does it align with Scripture? If I already have a theology, is it any good?

Perhaps a better place to start is even simpler: What is theology anyway?

Glad you asked.

What Is Theology?

Two years after that fateful day in my first theology class, I enrolled in Intro to Biblical Greek. I thought I might lose my mind.

Greek is all about memorization, and the seemingly endless vocabulary flashcards threatened my sanity on a daily basis. The class was comprised of mostly male students; myself and the spunky blonde sitting next to me were holding our own. And if it wasn't for Heather Joy—the intellectual powerhouse of a woman wrapped in a petite polka-dot dress and a single strand of pearls—I may have dropped the course. Heather Joy held my hand through Greek pop quizzes and late-night vocabulary cramming.

One of the first Greek vocabulary words that Heather Joy and I memorized was the Greek word for God, *Theos*. This word appears on just about every page of the New Testament, a prominent reminder of the God who spans the entire Bible. *Theos*, we always remembered, was the most common name for the God in Greek (which meant that if you remembered that vocabulary word, you were bound to get at least a 5% on any given exam).

Heather Joy and I found funny ways to remember just about every vocab word. We remembered *ego* was translated "I" by laughing about how big our egos were in high school; we memorized *kardia* as "heart" by remembering that cardiologists were medical heart specialists. Some of our mnemonic devices were better than others (and some were plain ridiculous, though they did the trick for the quiz the next day), but one will always stick with me. *Theos*, we recalled, is translated "God" because *theo*logy is the study of the Divine.

The Greek term behind the word *theology* is more revealing than it may initially seem. Theology has much less to do with charts and graphs than it does with the subject of its study: God. Theology is the study of God; or, more accessibly put, it is the pursuit of the knowledge of God. Theology begins with him and it ends with him. While we can think of a lot of fancy subsections of theological topics, put simply and precisely, *theology is our human pursuit to know God.*

And because theology starts with God, we find it branching out into every place God's presence and power reach. Because we want to know and understand God (to the extent that our limited, human minds are able), we want to know and understand everything God touches. This is why theology has grown in popular understanding to encapsulate what we believe about God *and* his world. In every place God shows up—across the globe, economy, relationships, and human nature—we want to seek to properly understand and articulate what God is up to, and who he has revealed himself to be.

You Are a Theologian, Too (Yes, *You*)

My professor was right. We are all theologians. Theology isn't reserved for academic books, but can be found anywhere a human heart beats. Boiled down to its fundamental nature, theology is what we believe about God, and we all believe something about him. Whether you were raised in the church and can piece together a good deal of factoids about God, are new to the Christian faith and find yourself barely able to articulate the basics of the gospel, or are an atheist who disbelieves in his existence—every person has a belief about the nature of God (or, in the atheist's case, his nonexistence). And, like I said before, that means each and every one of us has a theology.

For most of us, these beliefs have been formed by our families and churches, have developed over the course of our lifetimes, and have only been affirmed or disproven by our life circumstances. But no matter where our theology came from, the question we must face is the same question my professor posed to my freshman theology class: Is it any good? Christians profess that we believe in the God of the *Bible*, not the God of our imaginations or the God we'd prefer or the God other people have painted for us. And if we believe in the God of the Bible, this means we have to stop and ask ourselves: Is our view of God the view that the Scriptures proclaim from Genesis to Revelation? Or does it more closely resemble our own traditions, upbringing, values, and social circles?

C. S. Lewis puts it just about as bluntly as my professor:

> Theology is practical, especially now. . . . If you do not listen to Theology, that will not mean that you have *no* ideas about God. It will mean that you have a lot of *wrong* ones—bad, muddled, out-of-date ideas.[2]

It is imperative for us as Christians to stop relegating theology to seminaries and classrooms and embrace the reality that we are all theologians. Why? Because the longer we neglect our status as theologians the longer we will neglect our responsibility to question our default view of God and instead seek one that aligns with the Word of God. As long as we think we don't have a theology (or we're content with an unexamined one), the longer we will let unbiblical views of God rule in our hearts and minds, and we will miss out on the joy of knowing the God who has revealed himself in Scripture. While we leave our theology unquestioned, we're ultimately missing out—missing out on the gift of knowing God as he is, growing in articulating his character and nature gladly to others, reflecting his character more and more each day, and living into the reality of the gospel in our everyday lives.

Knowledge and Love

When I first met my husband, Austin, I liked him instantly. He was cool and sociable, the way very few first-year seminary students seem to be (if you know you know). He swiftly offered

---

[2] C. S. Lewis, *Mere Christianity* (New York: HarperCollins Publishers, 2017), 128, emphasis added.

to take my roommates and I hiking; he listened to good music; he was a good cook. I liked him, or at least I thought I did.

We became fast friends, Austin and I. We frequented the same coffee shop to study, where we'd have long conversations about life, family, friends, and our studies. He made an impression on me with his high integrity, deep compassion for others, and easy-going personality. And when he asked me on our first date, I had a feeling: I just might love him. But I was wrong.

Our season of dating was short and sweet. We had the absolute best time romping around the north shore of Boston, finding hole-in-the-wall fish shops that made the best lobster rolls, and visiting the Boston Museum of Fine Art. The more time we spent together, the more I learned about Austin's inner-workings: I noted how he approached decisions with discernment and caution, learned that finding parking makes his "top ten most-stressful to-do's" list, and heard from him how God called him to seminary and into ministry. And I loved him—or, at least, I thought I did.

After dating six months, Austin asked me to marry him and I undoubtably said yes. The following June we got married and moved into a little apartment on Main Street in Gloucester, Massachusetts. That first year of marriage I learned more about him than I ever had before—about his daily routines and habits, quirks and frustrations, insecurities, and deep strengths. And as I grew in understanding my new husband, the more I grew to love him. If you would have asked me then if I could love him more, I would have told you no. But, again, I would have been the fool.

Years, three cross-country moves, four job changes, and several financial highs and lows later found us standing together in a small bathroom in North Carolina waiting on the results of a pregnancy test. It was unexpected, unplanned, and I honestly didn't know how Austin would react. But I was soon to learn him in a new way: his eyes flashed sharply with joy when the result was positive. And I loved him all over again.

Each new chapter of this life together has brought new learning of each other. Our first night home from the hospital with our little one, our first Sunday of church planting, our ongoing attempts to resolve conflicts and forgive one another in the moments we fail each other, hard decisions and deepening friendships—each season has revealed more of our internal wiring, our personality quirks, and our character. And every season before that I thought I loved him now seems pale—like a blurry form of the love we now share—because knowledge fosters love.

Here is a fundamental truth: we cannot love what we do not know. There were other seminary classmates who I met the same time as Austin, but do I love them? Well, not really, and certainly not in any way similar to the way I love Austin. Why? Because I know Austin infinitely better than I ever got to know them. I have learned Austin over the years, and that knowledge of him has increased, fed, and fueled my love for him.

Knowledge of God, Worship of Him

We cannot love someone we do not know, and the same is true of God. For those of us who follow Jesus, the first spark of love for God we likely remember was either prior to our conversion (as we learned of God through the life of someone else and something inside us started slowly warming to the idea of him) or *at* our conversion. When we heard the good news of the gospel—the foundational reality of how God is at work in the world to save us, the lost—that spark grew into a flame. When we gave our lives to him, committing to follow him and inviting him to be Lord of our lives, our love solidified and took center stage, warming us through and sustaining our spiritual lives. As we have learned of him throughout our lives, we are likely to find our love growing in tandem.

Love is a powerful thing in the human heart. We will reorient our lives for people we love, relocate across miles and oceans to be with those we love, and sacrifice a great deal of personal comfort for those we hold in affection. Love is powerful.

In our spiritual lives, the way that love forms our behaviors and lives goes by another name: worship. Whatever holds the place of highest affection in our hearts is the object of our worship. We will wrap our lives and behaviors around it, we will change course and change our lives to honor it, we will let our love motivate us to transform even the most fundamental aspects of our personhood—and when we do, it is more than fondness showing up in our lives. This is worship.

The whole of the Christian life is worship of God. To be a Christian is to put a stake in the ground in terms of our highest affections, letting the God of the Bible lay claim on our hearts and lives in such a way that everything we are and everything we do wraps around our worship of him.

Worship isn't only what happens on Sunday mornings when we close our eyes and raise our hands as we sing; that is worship, but that is not all worship is. Worship is what happens when what we love shapes us—when we submit our character, choices, wills, and ways to God out of love and reverence for him. Worship is love for God that seeks to obey, honor, praise, and adore him; it is setting the eyes of our hearts on him in love and responsively lifting our faces toward him in awe and affection.

And because of this, it's fundamental that we seek to *know* God because love grows in the fertile soil of that knowledge (or, theology). Where knowledge grows, there love can grow too; where love flourishes, our worship will flourish in stride.

God's Pursuit of Us

There's good news for us. Our pursuit of God is not only met with God's pursuit of us, it is preceded by it. We worship a God who wants to be known by his people, who has sought out the lost children of his love and who has, time and time again, revealed himself to the world. We don't have to go on an academic excursion to grow as theologians; we simply have to open the Word of God and read everything he wants us to know about himself.

In fact, it's God who made the human heart a place of worship. You are divinely designed to worship someone or something. And he has oriented the world in such a way that knowledge and love work as co-operators of our human hearts. Though our human limitations make perfect knowledge of God impossible in our lives, God has seen fit to reveal himself to us so we can actually know true things about him. He has given us access to more knowledge of himself than we are entitled to; he has made aspects of his character, will, and ways accessible to us so we would grow in knowledge of him, foster love for him, and worship him as a result.

Nothing New

The connection between knowledge of God and our worship of him is not a new thing, but stretches all the way back to Genesis. On the earliest pages of Scripture we find our own human history, and as we read, we are pleased to be reminded of a time when the gap between human knowledge of God and God himself was scantest (or, when human theology was most whole). And their worship followed suit; because they knew God, their only experience of the world up to that point was one of unadulterated love and worship of their Creator.

Why was this the case in Eden? What made their knowledge of God and their worship of him so unhindered? He was *with* them. In Eden, knowing God simply meant opening your eyes.

The first man and woman beheld the object of their study and delight—of their theology and their worship—with their own two eyes. Because God was among them as their source and sustainer, their eyes were naturally fixed on him. As he revealed his character to them, they had no reason to shift their gaze; they had no reason to doubt, no need to disbelieve.

Until they did. The serpent, rightly called the deceiver, came with twisting words and a flattering tongue. God had told Adam and Eve not to eat of the Tree of the Knowledge of Good and Evil. And with their eyes on their Creator, they agreed—they had no reason to believe this good and gracious God would withhold any good thing from them. And at that very tree, the serpent whispered in the ears of God's people, "Did God really say?" *Was there knowledge God was withholding from them? Was there a better, more filling knowledge than knowledge of the God of their gaze?*

Eve's eyes flitted to the fruit.

The Bible tells us that she saw it was good for food and *delightful to her eyes.* She plucked it, she bit it, and she gave it to her husband who was right there with her. Immediately their eyes fell. Their necks bent over in a downward curve of self-protection as their eyes fixed on their own bodies—and they realized they were naked.

We know the rest of the story, not in least part due to the reality that we live within the confines of this story every day. God's people were banished from God's presence because they had fallen into sin, and sin has no place in the presence of a holy God. They could no longer look upon his face, no longer fix their eyes on his unblemished character. Sin had separated them from God—from knowing him as he is, and from knowing him personally and relationally. And, as a devastating result, their worship of him was corrupted; they could no longer know him as they once had, and their affections and worship toppled in tow.

East of Eden, knowledge of God was different. God, in his mercy and grace, continued to reveal himself to his self-focused people. He spoke to his people through angels and visions and prophets and poets. He related to them through burning bushes and clouds and tents and the temple. But they could not see him, nor could they know him fully (Exod. 33:20; Deut. 4:12).

And so, God's people clung (faithfully and fitfully) to the final words he spoke over Adam and Eve as they exited Eden:

one day, he would send a Savior who would crush the serpent and make a way for them to be in his presence again. One day, a Savior would come who would be to them the very representation of God's fullest glory (Heb. 1:3), would pay the penalty of death their sin deserved, and make them right with God again.

One day, God promised his self-gazing, inwardly bent creation, mankind would once again proclaim that they know God for they had *seen* him (1 John 1:1).

Living East of Eden

You and I also live east of Eden, but we live on the other side of this promise's fulfillment—we live our daily lives in the aftermath of God's promise kept in Christ. In Jesus, we know God's abundant faithfulness: he *did* bring the fullness of God's presence to earth, he *did* die our death and raise to life again so we might know God personally, fully, and relationally. In Christ, we are set free *from* love of self and freed *into* love of God; we are let loose from worship of self and invited, once more, into worshiping the God of the universe.

Today, we live our lives in the in-between, or what theologians call the "already-not-yet." Those of us who have placed our faith in Christ are *already* made right with God through Jesus, and we are *not yet* fully restored to the presence of God. And the ongoing work of the Spirit of God is to take our self-gazing selves and fix our eyes on Christ. In every place where the fall has bent us inward on ourselves—where we are self-fixated, self-admiring, self-concerned, self-reliant—the Holy Spirit powerfully, divinely, and generously lifts our chins to gaze upon the Son of our salvation.

The Christian life is lived out now in these spaces of turning from self to God. Not because "self" is altogether bad, but because it has no salvation in and of itself to offer us. Thus, the biblical call on our lives as followers of Jesus is not to seek *ourselves* and live, but to seek *God* and live (Amos 5:6)—to pursue knowing him as he truly is, and to live our lives in full submission, reverence, and worship of him. To surrender to God's sanctifying work is to say with the psalmist, *You, God, are the lifter of my head* (Ps. 3:3). To fix our eyes on him as we embrace his invitation to theological study and into responsive worship.

Modern Divorce

As we do this, we will find a decided division in ourselves and in our culture closing. Though God has wired us in such a way that knowledge leads to love and spills over into worship, we live in a fractured version of that reality. We have been saved from the penalty of our sin, but we have not yet been freed from the presence of sin. And this reality has dug a huge ditch between our knowledge of God and our worship of him. Where we should anticipate finding them working in tandem, we often find them segregated, detached, and divided.

Brokenness comes naturally for us as fallen humans, and so we shouldn't be surprised to find that we easily break the God-given harmony between theology and worship. Often, we emphasize one to the neglect of the other; identify ourselves as "theologically-minded" *or* as a heart-felt worshiper. A thinker after God's thoughts or a feeler after God's heart. Where God insists both—and, we often prefer an either-or approach.

And the results are devastating.

We see groups of believers delighting in studying doctrine and theology, who dive deeply into the things of God. But without worship as the end goal, temperaments grow rigid and joy grows dim. The theology that should naturally flow into worship is stopped short; and, with nowhere to go, the affection that should be cultivated either dries up or worse, turns inward. In this case, any affection cultivated is given to the self—a pat on our own backs for how much we know, pride that inevitably morphs into bitterness, anger, or smugness. When we emphasize theology (our study of God) and diminish doxology (our worship of him), we grow more concerned with getting the answer about God "right" than with allowing God to transform our hearts more and more into his likeness. Theology without worship may be accurate, but it cannot be affectionate; it may be correct, but it cannot be sweet.

Similarly, believers also occupy the opposite end of the spectrum. These people emphasize experience of God in worship without rooting their worship of God in what he has revealed about himself. Here, emotions run high and affections are deep, but, without proper theological roots, growth cannot come. We will very soon find ourselves seeking another spiritual high, curating environments that prick our emotions so that we can connect with God again. Worse, in our efforts to seek such an experience, we may even find ourselves in environments that teach questionable and even dangerous things about God, but in our ignorance of God's self-revelation, we do not recognize it. Doxology without theology lacks depth, growth, health, and support to sustain it over the long-haul.

Theology and Worship

Here's the good news in all of this: if the stakes are that high when we separate theology and worship, the stakes are equally high when they fall into proper alignment. When knowledge of God and worship of him work together as God designed, we will be Christians who know God *and* who love him; who learn about him *and* respond to what we are learning in worship; who do the hard work of studying the Scriptures that we might understand God as he has revealed himself *and* fall on our knees in surrender and affection before the God of the Bible. When we make both the study of God and our worship of him nonnegotiables, we have the chance to become the kind of Christians who know and love God with our whole selves.

Yet we cannot do this on our own. We need help.

You and I know the crevices of our hearts well: we like our know-it-all approach to theology, and find our spiritual highs in worship sweet. To bring both knowledge of God and worship of him back into harmony, we need someone to do a work within us. We need someone who will pull theology out of the abstract, put fresh pen to the paper of our hearts, and rewrite our desires until we heed the call to know and love God. And we need someone to take that desire, call it forth, fan that flame, and make our worship a more marvelous offering to God than we ever could on our own. In other words, we need an Author and we need a Perfecter for our faith.

His name is Jesus.

When the early church felt the same pull of sin and the weight of the fall, when they wondered how they should live out their daily lives as those who know and worship God, these words fell like a salve on their weary, wondering hearts:

> Let us also lay aside every encumbrance and the sin which so easily entangles us, and let us run with endurance the race that is set before us, *fixing our eyes on Jesus, the author and perfecter of faith,* who for the joy set before Him endured the cross, despising the shame, and has sat down at the right hand of the throne of God. (Heb. 12:1–2 NASB, emphasis mine)

Jesus is the one who gives shape and substance to our theology. He is the one who pulls theology out of the abstract and reveals it for what it was meant to be all along: knowledge of God that spills over into love for him. And it is Jesus who gives rootedness to our worship, grounding it in his character and nourishing it by his Spirit.

Friend, do you want to grow as a theologian (after all, you already are one)? Do you want to mature as a worshiper of God (after all, you will worship something)?

Fix your eyes on Christ.

He is the one who makes both theology and worship what they were meant to be. He alone is the revelation of God made manifest and the one due highest praise. And, it is his good and holy desire to reveal himself to you through his Word, foster love for God in your heart, and let it warm you through such that you live a life of worshipful discipleship and obedience with deep-running affection and reverence for God.

It is my aim to aid you in this journey, for it is one I'm taking myself. The road of knowing and loving God is one I am still walking, and by God's grace will walk for a very long time yet. But if you're up for it, I'd love to walk with you. What follows in this book is an attempt to help us bridge the gap between our doctrine and our discipleship, between our theology and our worship, between what we say we believe about God and what our lives actually look like.

In each subsequent chapter, we will consider a theological doctrine and seek to understand how it changes our daily lives of worship as we orient ourselves toward God. For example, we'll ask questions about how our theology of the trinity leads us to worship God as the Sanctifying One. We'll discuss the doctrine of the incarnation—when the Son of God became flesh in the person of Jesus Christ—and ask hard questions about what that means for our view of the human form and our call to a local body of believers. We'll look at what God teaches about his church, and the way that forms and shapes the ways we live in our homes, our neighborhoods, and our world.

In short, we will fix our eyes on Christ, inviting him to lead us into knowing and worshiping God. We will resist amassing for ourselves knowledge for the sake of pride, and instead, we will rush into the work of letting the knowledge of God find its feet in our daily lives of discipleship. We will lose our taste for base-less spiritual experience and will retrain our spiritual appetites to crave God's self-revelation and subsequent invitation into praise. We will repeatedly—over and over and over again like a holy liturgy—fix our eyes on Jesus until we find the divine design of our Creator operating in our redeemed human hearts, and can say with the psalmist:

> *I will study your commandments*
> *and reflect on your ways.*
> *I will delight in your decrees*
> *and not forget your word.*
> *(Ps. 119:15–16 NLT)*

Theology Proper:
Worshiping the God Who Is

Worship is pure or base as the worshiper
entertains high or low thoughts of God.[1]
A. W. Tozer

In high school, I was a self-professed Jesus freak. I fit every ste-
reotype of an impassioned youth grouper at a Baptist church.
I wore my tough faith on my sleeve, stood up for creationism
in biology class, and invited everyone in my math pod to youth
group. I even made my own T-shirt that said "Got Jesus" from
iron-ons I found at the local craft store. My whole life of faith,
if you would have asked me then, was wrapped up in one name:
Jesus.

I blush a little bit as I recount this. My sixteen-year-old self
was bold and brazen about faith. I pulled no punches in sharing
with others the hope I found in Christ. On the one hand, the
recollection makes me sheepish; how I wish I could remind my
younger self to extend more grace to others, season her words

---

[1] A. W. Tozer, *Knowledge of the Holy* (New York: HarperCollins,
1961), 1.

with gentleness, and invest in the long view of evangelistic relationships. On the other hand, as I think on my high school days,
a deep humility settles into my gut; God used that wild faith to
share the gospel with coworkers who worked the late shift at the
local hotel where I manned the front desk, and I can't help but
recall the lanky redhead from math class who took that invitation to youth group, came to know Jesus personally, and, as I
write this, has just completed his PhD in theology. God is bigger
than our failures or triumphs in faith—and that is a gift.

I look back on that time in my life and see a plethora of areas
in which I needed to grow (have I mentioned that I wore actual
pajama pants to school sometimes?), one area is glaringly obvious
to me: my faith, and the gospel message I proclaimed, was exclusively about Jesus. I named Jesus as my Savior, prayed to Jesus,
prayed in the name of Jesus, and shared the good news about
Jesus with others. To a certain extent, this is theologically true—
Jesus is the center of the gospel, the proclamation of the Word
of God and the Savior of the world! And yet, it also reveals a
theological immaturity; if someone were to call me a "God freak"
rather than a "Jesus freak," I can only imagine I would have been
offended. I was not a follower of "God"—I was a follower of
Jesus.

Who Is God?

I'm not alone in my Jesus-exclusive language about the
Christian faith. Maybe you would have joined me in thinking
of "God" as a generic term for the divine, and you would largely
prefer the specific name of Jesus be associated with your pursuit
of faith. The term *God* looms large with mystery—do we mean
any deity? Who or what exactly are we talking about when we
speak of "God" if we don't speak of him precisely in terms of
Jesus Christ?

Let me say this clearly: we can never over-emphasize Jesus.
He is the cornerstone, the Savior, God made flesh. I in no way

desire to communicate that we should give the person of Christ less attention, glory, or honor in our theology (as Michael Bird exclaims, "May it never be!"[2]). But there is a risk we run in our theological circles when we come to speak of God *only* in terms of Jesus. We threaten trading our proper Christo-centric theology (Christ-centered theology) for Christo-monic theology (Christ-only theology); and in doing so, we lose the very God-nature that makes Jesus such a glorious revelation of God himself.

We do well to start our theological journey with a question my high school theology failed to account for: Who is God? What do we mean when we speak of God himself? What does it mean to be divine? This is the theological context we need for everything that is to come—it will give shape to all we will explore about the Father, Son, and Spirit, the gospel, the church, the life to come, and more. It gives substance and structure to everything we believe about Jesus; not diminishing it, but elevating it to its proper height of joy and majesty. Or, as Bird puts it, "The doctrine of God is the galaxy in which the constellation of Christology is formed."[3]

If theology is the study of God, we first must ask: What do we mean by "God"? That is the question of Theology Proper.

Setting the Agenda

There are few things more irritating to me than a meeting without a clear agenda. You likely know the wearisome scenario: everyone dodders into the conference room or library or meeting room, gathers around a table, and readies themselves for what is at hand. But the problem is, no one seems to know what exactly is at hand. And because no one knows what this meeting is about, a general anxiety settles like fog on the group—*Did we*

---

[2] Michael F. Bird, *Evangelical Theology, Second Edition: A Biblical and Systematic Introduction* (Grand Rapids: Zondervan, 2020), 101.
[3] Ibid., 101.

do something wrong that our superior is gathering us to correct? Was I supposed to prepare something for this meeting? Will I be asked a question I don't know the answer to?

Without an agenda, everyone chats about what's on their mind, the project that's running behind and the ongoing stress everyone shares; someone is bound to share a story about a client interaction (almost always the long version) in attempts to fill the void of time and silence in the room. After about an hour, the person "leading" the meeting punctuates the eventual settling silence with a concluding question: *Well . . . anything else?*

No one knows what has been accomplished (was there anything to accomplish?), or what they're responsible for as they leave the meeting. Without an agenda, there is no way to tell if the meeting went well or poorly, if the team "got it right" or not, if we did the thing we came to do or not.

It's a de-motivating feeling, but there's good news: most of the time, the stakes aren't that high. An hour spent with coworkers or other parents from the school or ministry partners is hardly a waste of time, even if nothing objective was accomplished.

But the agenda at hand for us is different. We are setting out on a quest to know the God of the Bible; or, put in more explicit terms, to explore theology. If our theology underpins the whole of our lives of worship and discipleship, then the stakes are, in fact, quite high.

The question about who God is and what it means to be God sets the agenda for you and me. It's the foundational question that we must explore before we dive into particular theological topics like what the church is or how salvation works. If theology is a map that is leading us somewhere, then the doctrine of God is the boundary lines of that map. It tells us what—or who—we are talking about. Like a good agenda outlined for a fruitful meeting, the question of who God is outlines the theological task at hand.

In this chapter we will explore the doctrine of God. We'll ask what God is like, how we know who he is, and more. As we do, we are laying the foundation for what lies ahead—outlining the agenda for what is to come. Everything we will learn and every question we will ask flows from what we believe about God, who he is, and what kind of God he is discovered to be. Underneath all our theological exploration in the chapters to follow, we will continue to find our understanding of the doctrine of God tantamount.

What did Jesus come to do and be to us? How we answer this depends on who we believe God to be.

How does the Spirit fill believers? How we answer this depends on who we believe God to be.

What is the aim of the church? How we answer this depends on who we believe God to be.

What kind of world awaits believers in the life to come? How we answer this depends on who we believe God to be.

An Ancient Question with an Answer

Who is God? This question is not a new one. In fact, I can't name a single philosopher who hasn't attempted, at least in short, to address this human curiosity. Kant insisted God is the moral center of civilization. Plato taught that God is the *arche* (prime mover) of the universe. Aristotle wrote that God was the beginning "principle" of the world. Freud believed God to be a therapeutic illusion for those with poor father figures.

Indeed, the question of who God is isn't new. But we should not let the ancientness of the question or the multiplicity of answers convince us that it is a question without an answer. Neither the number of times this question has been asked nor the variants of answers given should dissuade us into thinking that it cannot be answered. It can be. It has been. There is an answer to who God is, and it is found in his holy Word.

As Christians, we are uniquely privileged to answer the question of who God is and what he is like with confidence, for our God, like I mentioned in the introduction, has revealed himself to us in the Bible. In Scripture, God has told us about himself, shared with us the contours of his divinity, expressed his character in ways we can understand and articulate, and has, in essence, given us the answer to our foundational question.

And the fact that he has done this tells us something about him already: he desires to be known! As we explore who God is, we are bound to run up against two realities that could discourage us in our theological journey: 1) the mysteries of God that we cannot fully understand in our human limitations, and 2) the complexities about God that, though understandable to the human mind, feel overwhelmingly big for ours. Theologian (because remember: you already are one!), when you bump up against either of these boundaries, call this to mind: your God desires to be known and has made himself known to you in his Word. He does not sit aloof in heaven, tapping his foot disappointedly because you cannot wrap your mind around his holiness; he is not evasive, trying to escape your understanding as if responding to your watchful eye with a game of divine whack-a-mole. Foundational to the Christian faith is this reality: the question of who God is has an answer because God is a God who desires to be known; in fact, he has given us everything we need to love, worship, and enjoy him in this life.

The Attributes of God

Our answer to the question of who God is lies within the pages of Scripture. There, we find a plethora of descriptions and examples of certain realities at play in God's character; theologically, these are called "attributes." When we ask who God is or what he is like, we're really hounding after his attributes—what are the contours of his character? What qualities make him who he is? What features belong to his divine being? Is he mean or kind? Is he fickle, fair, friendly?

After grappling with all that the Bible says about God, theologians separate these attributes into two lists: *communicable* and *incommunicable.* Let's start with *communicable.* These are the attributes in God's character that we have unique access to as humans made in his image. These attributes are "communicable" to us in that they can be transmitted to us, or shared with us; they are characteristics that belong to God that can also belong to us. For example, God is merciful and he calls us to be merciful; God is just and he commands us to live justly. These are the things that allow the Bible to say we bear God's likeness in certain ways.

But there are also attributes of God that belong to him alone. These aspects of his character and nature are "incommunicable" to us as humans. We do not possess them, and we never will simply because we are not God. An example of an incommunicable attribute (which we will unpack at greater length shortly) is his omniscience, or his all-knowing nature. God alone has all knowledge and wisdom within himself; he neither commands nor expects us to become like him in this way. Similarly, God is self-sufficient; he relies on no one and nothing to sustain his divine self, and the same could never be said for you and me. These attributes do not communicate to our human nature; he does not share them with us—they are God's incommunicable attributes, and they are the reason the Bible says there is no one like him. In short, you could say the communicable attributes connect us to God, while the incommunicable attributes set him apart from us, drawing the line between creature and Creator. On one hand, considering the communicable attributes, it is clear that we are like God to a degree much like a child bears the image of his parent. On the other hand, considering the incommunicable attributes, it is clear God is something (Someone) entirely different than we are.

Differently Similar

I married into owning the cutest pup in the entire world. Our golden retriever, Penny Lane (named after the Beatles' song), is a key member of the Gannett family. Penny Lane is always up for

running in the yard, going for a hike, or slumbering at home, and
given her natural love for eating, napping, and playing on repeat,
I often joke that she is my spirit animal.

But Penny and I didn't always get along. In her puppy days,
there were ways that she operated that were incompatible with
my own. The way she played in her water bowl and soaked the
kitchen floor, for example, was not my idea of a good time. As
I didn't want to be the diva newlywed who kicked the dog off
all the furniture, I asked Austin to sit down and work with me
to create an outline of the way we wanted our home to be, particularly in terms of how Penny would relate to that home. The
list we created was simple: our home would be peaceful, patient,
welcoming, and more.

This meant that Penny needed to learn from us how to live
into these attributes of our home. Because our home was to be
peaceful, Penny learned not to bark. Because our home was a
place of patience, Penny learned to wait at the door to go out and
to wait by her bowl for dinner. Because our home was a welcoming place, Penny learned to greet our friends gently rather than
viewing them as suspect (or salivating her love all over them).

There were aspects of who Austin and I are that we instilled
in Penny Lane—by teaching her, by being with her, and by exem-
plifying these traits, Penny learned to mirror them. And yet . . .
in so many ways, Penny will never become like us. She is patient,
but she is not human. She is welcoming, but she will never shake
hands with our guests and ask, "How do you do?"

The metaphor is imperfect. God does not view us like dogs
to be trained, and he is certainly much more to us than a benevolent owner. And we did not transmit these traits into the inner
fabric of our dog by way of creating her. But the illustration captures for us a glimpse of reality: God is entirely different from
us. He has an entirely other nature and is a being to which he
can only compare himself. These, his incommunicable attributes,
limit our view and emulation of him. So if you find yourself puz-
zling at his immutability or wondering at his omnipresence, then

you're in the right frame of mind; we can no more wrap our minds around the entirety of who God is than Penny Lane can fully articulate what it means to be human.

And yet, God is not unknowable. Just as Penny learned to emulate attributes that belonged to Austin and me, so we are invited, by the power of God's Spirit, to grow in his commutable attributes. Though we know not the experience of being a limitless being and cannot even comprehend what it means that God is eternal, by his good design, we are invited to live in what we will come to know as the "economy of the household of God" and therein learn to mirror his communicable attributes.

For the rest of this chapter we will consider God's incommunicable attributes and communicable attributes, in that order. For sake of clarity and conciseness we will consider a list of eight from each category, knowing the conversation goes far beyond what will be said in the following few pages. Our aim here is to see these from a five-thousand-foot perspective as we ask and answer the question: *Who is God?*

Incommunicable Attributes

We are not God. Therein lies our greatest hope.

The incommunicable attributes of God will show up in a thousand theological places in the coming pages—both in big and small ways. The reality of a Christian God who is unlike any other is a foundation for our doctrine and the baseline of our theology. The fact that God is in a category of his own is actually what creates our theological pursuit—it is the reality that surges in our hearts a desire to know and articulate what we can about him! As we unpack eight of God's incommunicable attributes, this is the truth we are savoring: there is no one like our God.

Infinite

God has no limits. He has no constraints, and he cannot be weighed or measured. In his being and essence, he is endless.

It is natural for children to think of God as being "bigger" than themselves; sometimes, we adults fall into this line of thought as well. But that actually doesn't capture the reality of God's infiniteness. God is not just bigger than us or bigger than we can imagine; he is a God with no boundaries, a God to which no dimensions or scales could be attempted. Though we can hop on a scale and weigh our members, or stand against a door frame and trace our childhood growth, the same cannot be said of God. In both his being and his essence, he is infinite.

To say that God is infinite is to say that God is beyond our greatest thoughts of him, he is higher and longer and wider and deeper than we can even conceive—and to ever speak in such measurable terms gives us away! This is why the book of Job referred to these things as the "deep things of God": God's nature and being lies far beyond the limitations of our human minds.

> "Can you find out the deep things of God?
>   Can you find out the limit of the Almighty?
>   It is higher than heaven—what can you do?
>   Deeper than Sheol—what can you know?
>   Its measure is longer than the earth
>   and broader than the sea." (Job 11:7–9)

Incomprehensible

God is beyond our human comprehension. Because there is none like him, he is unfathomable in his nature, inscrutable in his knowledge, and incomprehensible in his work.

The infinite nature of God leads us directly to his incomprehensibility. Because we humans are limited creatures, we have limited imaginations and minds and understanding, much like a child at the tender age of three cannot possibly grasp the full scope of her parent's wisdom, love, and so on. It isn't wrong for the child to not understand everything, of course, but the gap between a parent and child is still quite wide. It should not surprise us that God's full nature lies beyond the boundaries of our mind's grasp. If the gap between a three-year-old and her parent is somewhat wide, the gap between us and God may as well be the width of the Grand Canyon to an infinite power. Who he is in his fullness cannot be captured in our minds or articulated in our words. He is in a category entirely his own.

God, in his fullness, is incomprehensible. And perhaps this reality causes you to pause; why then, did you pick up a theology book at all? If we cannot fully know God, why study the nature of God? The answer is simple: just because God cannot be fully known does not mean he cannot be sufficiently known.[4] God, in his glorious humility and desire for his creation to know him, gives us sufficient knowledge of himself—both that we might be saved, and that we might spend our entire lives seeking to know him more without ever coming to the end of our pursuit. There will always be more to discover about him.

Aseity

God relies on no one and nothing. He alone is self-sufficient and self-existent. He does not derive life from any source outside of himself; he does not need to, for he "has life in himself" (John 5:26).

I have always considered myself an independent person. But in theological terms, that self-conception is laughable. I require food to sustain my life, sleep to maintain my body, and oxygen to fill my lungs. A very brief survey finds me dependent on a plethora of things simply to survive (not to mention to thrive).

But God is wholly other. God has need of nothing apart from himself. God is the only true independent, the only one who is, in his essence, autonomous. He was not created by any other source or power or person—he has existed for all time, on his own, without the support or supply of another. He is transcendent, existing by his own power, dependent on nothing but

---

[4] Jen Wilkin, *None Like Him: 10 Ways God Is Different from Us (and Why That's a Good Thing)* (Wheaton, IL: Crossway, 2016), 34.

himself. This is why the Bible opens with such an assumptive first line: "In the beginning, God . . ." There was no cause to the One who caused the first activity of the universe; there was no creator for the One who created the world. He always has been and he always will be completely, eternally, and perfectly self-sufficient and self-existent.

Immutable and Impassible

God does not change. Who he is in his nature, character, and essence is eternally the same.

God does not grow and evolve as we speak of people doing. Though we may look at our friends and family members, reminiscing about ways they used to be, hair styles they used to have, opinions they used to hold passionately (thank the good Lord I no longer wear pajama pants in public). But the same kind of conversation cannot be applied to God. He does not change. From eternity past, he has remained the same. This is God's immutability.

God's impassibility works in tandem with it. While his immutability speaks to the big-picture conversation about God's unchangeability (his nature, essence, being, character, etc.), God's impassability sets him apart from humans when it comes to our proclivity to change in response to our daily experiences. God is not given over to passions (hence his *im*passible nature). Unlike us, His emotions don't ride a roller coaster, and he isn't given over to temper tantrums. He is eternally the same.

Omnipotent

God is all-powerful. There is nothing that is too hard for him (Gen. 18:14). No words can be uttered by God that will be devoid of power; when God speaks, all of creation does his bidding (Isa. 55:11).

The prefix *omni* simply means "all," so when we speak of his omnipotence, we are speaking of his all-powerful (or all "potent") nature. This is a particularly difficult concept for us to wrap our minds around because there are, of course, things God cannot do. God cannot act contrary to his nature, which means he cannot lie (Titus 1:2). He also cannot do things that are logically contradictory, like creating a rock so big he cannot lift it. (When we start asking these kinds of questions of God's all-powerful nature, we do well to revisit his incomprehensibility!)

So what do we mean when we say God is omnipotent? When we say God is all-powerful, we are saying that God has total *control* over all things.[5] The Bible teaches us that this includes the smallest elements of our daily lives, like the hairs that grow on our heads and the sparrow that falls from the sky (Matt. 6:26–30; 10:29–30), to the grandest reality of our known world like establishing kings and rulers (Isa. 44:28), and which ones will rise and fall (Ps. 33:10–11). In God's all-powerful nature, he knits together human DNA in the womb (Ps. 139:13–16) and saves sinners from eternal death, extending them his powerful grace and saving life in his Son (Eph. 2:8–10). There is nothing beyond God's power; no act too difficult for him. As he says through the mouth of a prophet: "Behold, I am the LORD, the God of all flesh. Is anything too hard for me?" (Jer. 32:27).

Omniscient

God is all-knowing. All knowledge belongs to him and originates with him.

The very fact that you are holding this book in your hands is a reminder that you are not God. In fact, in terms of your knowledge (and mine), you are totally unlike him. Where humans must learn in order to gain knowledge, God has never needed to learn anything for all knowledge is his. No one is his teacher; there is no book that can instruct him. There is nothing beyond his comprehension—whether in the past or the present or the future.

---

[5] John M. Frame, "The Omnipotence, Omniscience, and Omnipresence of God," *The Gospel Coalition*, www.thegospelcoalition.org/essay/omnipotence-omniscience-omnipresence-god/.

There is nothing he does not already know. All knowledge is God's.

God's knowledge isn't simply factual but personal. It would be one thing if God simply knew all there was to know about math (which, of course, he does because math and numbers are the invention of his limitless mind); but God's knowledge is more than factoids or fields of discipline. It is also intimate. What do I mean? God knows not only how his own world works, but also the innermost realities of every being that lives in that world—including you and me. Have you ever felt cornered by someone who outlined the way you usually operate? Maybe it was the results of a personality test or leadership profile that left you feeling boxed in by others' knowledge of you. Let a deeper reality settle into your heart: God knows the depth of you. He knows how you operate and why, but beyond that, he knows your heart and, in fact, knows it better than you do (Jer. 17:10; Ps. 44:21; Prov. 15:11; John 2:24–25; 1 John 3:20). There is no limit to God's knowledge.

Omnipresent

There is nowhere God is not present. He is not limited to being in one place at a time, but is present at all places at all times. He's everywhere.

I have often stood at the kitchen sink wishing I could be in just one more place at a time. If I could only run errands while also getting the house cleaned up, I'd finally have time to answer those work emails. But my very best attempts at multitasking only serve to remind me of my human limit to be in a single place at a time.

But this is just not true of God. He is the God of no limits, as we've already seen, and this applies to his presence as well. God is all-present. There is no place off limits to him, and there is no threshold to the number of places he can simultaneously be. By God's power and knowledge, he is present in every place and time. This is why the psalmist exclaims in Psalm 139,

Where shall I go from your Spirit?
   Or where shall I flee from your presence?
If I ascend to heaven, you are there!
   If I make my bed in Sheol, you are there!
If I take the wings of the morning
   and dwell in the uttermost parts of the sea,
even there your hand shall lead me,
   and your right hand shall hold me.
(vv. 7–10)

Sovereign

God's lordship extends into all areas of the universe. There is no place where God does not possess total and right authority and rule.

Having surveyed God immutable and incomprehensible, God self-sufficient and self-existent, God all-powerful, all-knowing and all-powerful, it should not surprise us that he is also totally and perfectly sovereign over his creation. The doctrine of God's sovereignty speaks to his rightful place as King over creation—and that he is. As a result of who he is in his nature and what he does in his acts toward men, God is on the throne of the universe. His authority is unrivaled.

Lest we mistake God's place of sovereign rule over creation as a throne *we* set him on, this doctrine is not the result of a democracy. God hasn't campaigned for the place of universal authority, listing his incommunicable attributes as the traits that would make him a fitting king. We are not voting on whether or not God takes the position of unrivaled ruler; it belongs to him. Authority is his because he is the author of all.

If this sounds a little scary, it's likely because, like me, you have seen authority go awry in human relationships. The pastor who doubles down on his position of authority when lovingly confronted with sin; the parent who inflicts harsh punishment on a child to make her succeed; the boss who can't keep a team together because of his bullish or authoritarian approach to the workplace. In human hearts and lives, unquestioned authority goes bad quickly.

But God's sovereignty, like all of his other attributes, is tied into one another. They are all perfectly who God is—which is why God's authority in creation is what leads him to the sacrifice of the cross, the power of the resurrection, and the rule in the new creation (all of which we will unpack in due time). God wields his sovereignty in ways congruent with all his other attributes. He rules, yes, *with goodness*. He reigns, indeed, *with mercy*. He governs, yes, *with justice*. He's an uncorrupted King with a kind hand, wisely directing all that goes on in the Universe.

Communicable Attributes

It would be easy to survey the list of incommunicable attributes and think of God as an alien of sorts—something or someone we cannot understand, relate to, or know in any real sense of the word. (And just think—we only looked at *eight* of his incommunicable attributes; there are many more!) But though God is in a category of his own, he has seen fit to create us in such a way that we are able to understand, relate to, and even emulate aspects of his nature. As we've already learned, these attributes are called God's communicable attributes, and they fill out the picture for us of a God we can follow, mirror, and imitate. If God's incommunicable attributes cause us to glory at how far beyond us God is, his communicable attributes are what cause us to revel that he draws and calls us so far into relationship with himself that we can be like him in these ways.

In each of the eight communicable attributes we will look at, we will find two truths at play: first, God is supreme in each of the categories. God is holy and invites us to be holy as well, but God alone remains *most holy*. God is good and invites us to be good, but God alone is *most good*. Though we can emulate these aspects of his character, we will never match the quality or extent to which these attributes exist in his being.

The second truth we will see is that we are invited to emulate these aspects of God's character, *and* he makes the power to do so available to us by his own Spirit. Though these attributes are accessible to us, and were once the way we naturally operated before the fall, sin has made them feel *unnatural* to us. We can only emulate God's character by the renewing work of his Spirit that teaches us to say "yes" to God and "no" to ways incongruent with God's perfect character (Titus 2:12).

Holy

God possesses absolute moral purity. He is perfectly perfect in his nature, will, ways, and character.

This aspect of God's nature is so important that the angels and cherubim around the throne repeat it as a triune anthem, and repeat it for all eternity: "Holy, holy, holy is the LORD Almighty" (Isa. 6:3 NIV). God's holiness means that he is ultimately perfect in his purity. There is no spot, blemish, shadow, or wrinkle in his character. He is perfectly perfect.

God does not sin—never has and never will. But God does not simply keep a perfect code perfectly; he defines it. He is not measuring up to some universal standard of righteousness; God *is* the ultimate standard of righteousness and perfection.

God's holiness is something that puts us in awe, and makes us quake in our boots—and rightfully so. It's God's holiness that makes him entirely *other* in his character. It is his holiness that creates such a stark divide between us and him (we'll get into this more in coming chapters). Because God is holy and we are sinful, we cannot look upon him without rightly fearing death (Exod. 33:19–23).

Does it seem like holiness should be relocated to the list of incommunicable attributes? God's command to "be holy, because I am holy" (1 Pet. 1:16) initially seems like an impossibility—and if we are thinking it is something we have to attain to in our own efforts, we are right. But that is not the gospel. The hope God offers us in that, in Christ, we are made holy by Christ's holiness, and we are invited into a life of becoming more and more holy as the Spirit sanctifies us and makes us like the God of our salvation. The call of the Christian life is a call from being dead in sin to being alive in Christ; being saved by God from depravity into *holiness*.

Good

God is perfectly virtuous. It is in his nature to be righteous, kind, and upright in all he does—from eternity past and into eternity future.

One of my favorite past times is thrift shopping. I love stumbling through warehouses full of wobbly-leg chairs, mismatched glassware, and old tufted couches. More often than not, my patience is rewarded when I come upon a true gem: something that was once considered very good, has seen some signs of wear or decay, but something that I have a vision to make very good once again. With a little wood stain, a little reupholstering, a little polishing of the brass, I can fill my home with thrifted treasures.

This journey from good to not-so-good and back again is a human experience. We see it in our own character—created very good, fallen into sin, and redeemed and sanctified by Christ—and see this progression scattered throughout creation. But this can never be said of God. God has always been perfectly, indisputably good. When he created the world and pronounced creation "good" and mankind "very good," he did so out of an overflow of his own character and nature. God himself is very good, and everything he does and is and wills is fit to match.

Unlike us, God goes through no progressions of goodness. He does not improve from good to better to best, for he has always been perfectly good. He does not get better with age or better himself with personal development; from eternity past and into eternity future, God is perfectly good.

God's holiness tells us something about where we get our human standards of morality and perfection; God sets that standard. But God's goodness takes this conversation a step further—God is not only the standard of moral purity, but he is benevolent in all that he does. From top to bottom, God is *good*. He is a fountain of generosity (James 1:5; John 3:16) and one in whom there is only light and not a spot of darkness (1 John 1:5), and he invites us, by the power of his Spirit, to live the same way.

Truthful

God is perfectly honest and trustworthy. Everything he says will come to pass, and he himself is the origin of truth.

Until recent generations, truth has generally been considered an objective reality. And that is what it is. Truthfulness is something that could be measured against an authoritative standard. If someone was lying or misleading, their words could be weighed and measured against the truth; individuals and organizations gained reputations for being misleading or forthcoming by how their words and actions coincided with the reality of truth.

Nothing weakens an objectively powerful word like *truth* like putting the word *your* in front of it. This has been the embarrassing habit of my generation: removing a standard of authority against which our beliefs and words can be measured, and dissolving into mealy-mouthed subjective statements like, "well, if that's *your* truth . . ."

This perspective won't hold up and it won't last. Why? Because there is a standard and arbiter of truth: God. God is the origin and establisher of truth. What he declares to be true is eternally and unchangingly true. Everything God says and does flows from his most truthful character. Because he is fully, eternally, and unchangingly true, God is incapable of lying.[6]

God's most truthful character means that he is 100 percent trustworthy; what he says will come to pass, is certain to come to pass. The promises he speaks are bound to be fulfilled. And God invites us to mirror this aspect of his character, urging us to

---

[6] Jen Wilkin, *In His Image: 10 Ways God Calls Us to Reflect His Character* (Wheaton, IL: Crossway, 2018), 123.

let our "yes be yes, and your no be no" (James 5:12) and to speak truthfully with our neighbors (Eph. 4:25).

Just

God is the standard of fairness and equity. There is no impartiality in him; he is perfectly just.

In his good and holy character, God has the authority to set the boundaries of morality, to declare who has and has not maintained those boundaries, and establish the consequences for failing to keep his standard. We see this beautifully on display in the Old Testament Law: God established a code of conduct for his people that made provisions for their sinfulness. God, taking into account his own holy perfection and his people's fallenness, gave his people the Law as a way for them to be in relationship with himself and as an invitation to mirror his character. The Law was an expression of God's justice and his own authority to determine what the laws should be and what the repercussions would be for those who fail to keep his laws.

God loves his law—both the Old Testament Law, and the commands laid out throughout the Old and New Testaments—and his law is perfectly fair. Though our limited human perspective may cause us to question the uprightness of God's judgments, the Bible declares that God is the only righteous and just Judge, and that he sits on a throne of impartiality and justice (Deut. 32:4). He is the kind of eternal Judge that cannot be bought or swayed; he cannot dole out a sentence unbefitting of the crime. In his eternal character, he has no bias that tints his actions or pronouncements; he is perfectly just from end to end (Isa. 30:18).

God's justice has a long view: in the end, no one gets away with anything. There is no unrighteous action, word, or motive of the heart that God's all-knowing mind does not perceive and that his perfectly just character will not judge.

This attribute of God's is good news for us if we have been victims of injustice. God's command and design for his creation is for us to emulate his justice so that the poor are not oppressed but lifted up, and so that lawbreakers are rightly punished and removed from positions of power (Isa. 1:17). But it may surprise us to find that this attribute of God's is also good news for us if we have ever been unjust. Where we have broken God's law and concealed it, where we have taken a bribe at the expense of our neighbor, where we have cheated for selfish gain—we will not get away with one ounce of it. Here is the good news of God's justice: although we are called to mirror God's justice to the world, we have failed, and so God took it upon himself to be the justifier—the one who literally makes us stand justly before the Father—in the sending of the Savior. God's justice was satisfied at the cross, and the new life offered us in Jesus opens the way for us, by the power of the Spirit, to "do justice, and to love kindness, and to walk humbly with your God" (Mic. 6:8).

Merciful

The heart of God is eternally kind and gracious. It is in God's nature to extend forgiveness and pardon sins. God's mercy culminated in the person of Christ.

Where God's justice determines that each person's sins get exactly what they deserve, God's mercy compels him to spare us what we rightly deserve, not by sweeping our sins under the rug as if they aren't there, but instead, pouring out the punishment for those sins on the willing head of his Son. Ever since the Edenic fruit was picked and bitten, God would be just to demand our lives and eternally separate us from himself. But he hasn't. He has, instead, extended us mercy—giving us length of days on this earth, signs that point us to our need for a Savior, and the proclamation that the only Savior who can save us is his own Son (whom, in his mercy, he sent to suffer in our stead). God's mercy is his active compassion toward us and toward the world he loves. In his mercy, he spares us from punishment (Ps. 86:5), extends salvation to us while we are dead in our sins (Eph. 2:4–5), and comforts us in our sorrows (2 Cor. 1:3).

God is eternally merciful. In fact, Scripture says that God is "rich" in mercy; if his mercy were a bank account, it would be overflowing. There is no poverty in God's storehouses of mercy. He extends compassion to his creation, shows grace to the hurting and lost, and is tenderhearted toward his people. And yet— we have no claims on his mercy. We harbor no entitlement to his compassion and have no right to insist he give us anything other than what we justly deserve. Though God is eternally merciful, he shows mercy according to his will (Rom. 9:18) and gives compassion as is fitting for his eternally just, eternally good character (Rom. 9:15).

While we have no claims on God's mercy, God has claims on ours. Because we have been shown mercy, God calls us to extend this mercy to others. Like the debtor forgiven much, we are compelled by God's forgiveness to extend mercy and forgiveness to others (Matt. 18:21–35). We have been forgiven, and God commands us to forgive (Col. 3:13); we have been shown God's mercy, and God commands us to likewise be merciful (James 2:13).

Loving

God is infinitely benevolent toward his people. God's heart of love stirs for his people, desiring to bestow upon them both physical and spiritual benefits—the chief of which is Jesus Christ.[7]

It is in God's eternal nature to love. God has, since before time began and before he breathed creation into existence, been a Father loving his Son (John 3:35; more on this in chapter 2 on the Trinity). In his love, he created and sustains his very good creation, and when those who bear his image fell into sin, in his love, he sent his Son to be the Savior of the world (John 3:16). It is in God's love that he effectively calls the lost into saving

---

[7] Sam Storms, "The Love of God," *The Gospel Coalition*, www.thegospel coalition.org/essay/the-love-of-god/.

relationship with himself, and in love for his people that he walks with us, provides for us, and brings us into his own joy as we walk in his ways (Jude 21; John 15:9–10; Ps. 103:9–18).

Love is so inherent to the character of God that Jesus summed up the law of God (remember the law that embodies his heart of justice?) in two commands. When asked which of the righteous commands of the law were the most important, Jesus responded this way:

> *Jesus answered, ". . . you shall love the Lord your God with all your heart and with all your soul and with all your mind and with all your strength." The second is this: "You shall love your neighbor as yourself." (Mark 12:29–31)*

The love we have received from God compels us into love for God and love for our neighbor. If God's love can take him to the cross and empty grave, then God's love can take us from loving only ourselves to loving God and others. God's love isn't a weak and wimpy thing of Hollywood movies; it's the powerful, life-changing attribute of God that we experience in salvation and are called to emulate in the life of the Spirit.

Faithful

God is endlessly trustworthy. Every promise and covenant he has made, he will keep—God is most faithful.

I am not known for my endurance. I am easily excited by new projects, only to quickly abandon them when something newer and more exciting comes along. To my projects (and sometimes shamefully to my promises regarding said project), I am unfaithful. But this has never been true of God. God is eternally faithful. What he has promised, he will see through; just as with God's truthfulness, anything he says he will do. He has never gone back on what he said or made a commitment he has not kept. God is most faithful.

The fidelity of God is put gloriously on display in his covenants. Being a relational God, he has always desired to have a relationship with his creation. Though sin separated us from God (both in terms of proximity and in terms of relational accessibility), God demonstrated his eager desire to be in covenant relationship with people (Adam, Noah, Abraham, Moses, David). In these covenants, God generously initiates a relationship with his people, joyfully binding himself to them in committed relationship and inviting his people to depend on him.

The Bible is one long true tale of God's faithfulness in the face of his people's faithlessness. Time and again, God's people break the covenant he has extended to them; they disobey his law, worship idols, and grieve his Spirit. And yet, despite their unfaithfulness, God is enduringly steadfast (Deut. 7:9). He maintains unswerving and steadfast faithfulness to them and to his covenant. Even now, in the New Testament church, where we are unfaithful to walk in the Spirit, to bear the fruit of righteousness, and to forsake our sin, God remains faithful (2 Tim. 2:13; 1 Thess. 5:24). There is not a hint of infidelity in God's character, not a speck or spot of flightiness. He will not abandon us; he is a faithful God.

God commands his people to be faithful because he is faithful. This command includes keeping our promises in ways that are consistent with his promise-keeping character (Heb. 13:4) and in holding with unswerving hope to the promises of God (Heb. 10:23). Because we worship God most faithful, we are invited to mirror his enduring fidelity in our own relationships, character, and lives.

Wise

God's established order for creation is a display of his all-wise nature. God's ways and commands are expressions of his good will toward mankind and originate in his eternally wise character.

There are laws written into the foundations of the world, and they are a result of God's creative work. When God created, he put his very nature into his work, and wrote the laws of our universe in such a way that points mankind to God and gives him glory. These laws are an overflow of God's most wise character (Prov. 3:19; 8:22–31). In his infinite wisdom, God ordained our human limitations and set our boundaries (Ps. 16:6); God wisely saw fit to embed creation with reminders that he is God and we are not, and there is none besides him (Exod. 34:14; Ps. 115:5).

The wisdom of God is not only written into the order of creation, it was also made flesh. The pinnacle of God's wisdom is the embodied Savior, Jesus Christ. Jesus came to put into motion God's redemptive plan and is to us the "wisdom of God" (1 Cor. 1:24). The truest wisdom we can name in this world is gospel wisdom—the message of salvation that God has "lavished upon us, in all wisdom and insight" (Eph. 1:8).

In Scripture, wisdom is personified as a woman crying out in the streets—but she's not just hollering, she is extending a divine invitation. What is she inviting people into? She beseeches them to fear God. The fear of the Lord, she assures them, is the beginning of walking in wisdom (Prov. 9:10).

The fear of God, biblically speaking, is holy reverence for God's character, will, nature, and ways, the chief of which is his Son, Jesus. It is this kind of bone-deep esteem for God that leads us into full-throttled belief that his ways are for our good, and to surrender the throne of our lives to Christ.

A Glimpse, Not an Expert (but also, an heir)

Some of my favorite early childhood memories are of meeting my dad at his dental office for lunch. About once a month, as my memory serves, my mom would tote me and my siblings up to my dad's dental clinic where we would share a lunch in his office. Walking through the front door, all the staff would oooh and ahhh over me. They'd compliment my dress or my new-to-me Mary Janes; they would ask me what I liked about first grade, and they always let me pick out what color toothbrush I wanted. They would let me browse the sticker case, and if I didn't find one I wanted, they'd show me the huge stash of them in the storage room. They let me sit in vacant operatory chairs and gave me "rides" by raising and lowering the seat backs. I have exactly zero memories of waiting in the waiting room while they called my dad to tell him I had arrived; the minute I walked into the office, I was whisked behind the door, toured through the staff offices, and delivered to my dad who was waiting for me. I was dental-office famous.

I so loved being at the office and eating lunch with my dad that I continued the habit into high school and college. If ever I had a free period in high school that overlapped with lunch, or if I was home from college on a holiday break, I would pick up fast food or pack two sandwiches, and eat across from him for a few minutes while he was between patients. And every time I walked through those doors it was, in a unique way, like arriving at a second home.

From my earliest memories, I was fully welcomed into my dad's office (I even knew where the bubble gum toothpaste was kept!). It *felt* to me like a second home, but I had no idea what all went on in the operation of a state-of-the-art dental clinic. Every visit there was a glimpse of my dad's world, and while I was invited in and welcome there, I by no means was an expert in his business operations. You could have asked me how to get to my dad's office from the front or where to find the surplus of stickers, but how to perform a root canal? How to handle payroll? How to keep inventory of medical supplies and machinery? That was all entirely beyond me.

When we survey God's incommunicable and communicable attributes—which we did with incredible brevity—we must realize two coinciding realities: we are welcome here to survey the character of God, but we are by no means becoming experts in his nature. In our human limitations, we cannot fully grasp the expansiveness of God; our minds cannot wrap themselves around his limitless character. We can sense when we're in his good presence, and we enjoy it (indeed, we should!) and even feel at home, but that doesn't mean we have him all figured out. He is in a category unto himself and there is none like him. We would be as foolish to claim full understanding of God as my seven-year-old self would have been to offer to fill a cavity for one of my dad's patients. God is entirely beyond us.

And yet this truth joyfully coexists alongside it: we are welcomed in. God has invited us, through his Word, to know him. Through our study of Scripture, we can know who he is, what he is like, and, perhaps most staggering of all, we can *know* him. His invitation isn't just to a head full of factoids about him, but into knowing him relationally and personally. In the Word of God, we get a glimpse of God's nature and it is enough to catapult us into intimate worship of him (Ps. 100:3).

What's the Point?

When we survey the expansiveness of God and when we acknowledge how much we cannot and do not know about God, you might start to wonder—why would we study the topic at all? Why commit our entire lives to being equipped as theologians if, in the end, we only get a glimpse of his nature? What is the point of going, time and again, to the Word if we cannot claim true expertise this side of heaven?

The point is this: you were invited to lunch with your dad.

Sure, you're just seven years old and unable to fully comprehend (not to even mention participate in) the day-to-day operations of a clinic. But your dad invited you. The door is open to you. The point isn't that you become the expert; the point is that his invitation to know him and his world is open to you—and, don't you want to walk through it?

We accept God's invitation to know him more through his Word because he has, in his vast love and affection, invited us.

God has made himself, albeit in part, knowable to you, and is extending the opportunity for you to commune more and more with him as you grow in theological understanding. It's not about one book or one class or one theological topic; it's about the fact that *you get to know and enjoy your God, Savior, and King.* It's about the habit of showing up time and again to get to know God, honoring him with our time, growing in affectionate worship for him, and loving him in response by our attentiveness, mindfulness, awe, and gratitude for his self-revelation. (You can even bring a sandwich, and you'll have no questions from me.)

The Trinity: Worshiping God Triune

> Indeed, in the triune God is the love
> behind all love, the life behind all life, the
> music behind all music, the beauty behind
> all beauty and the joy behind all joy.[1]
>
> *Michael Reeves*

We pulled up behind our real estate agent. I let out an audible gasp. In front of us was a little white ranch-style house, neatly framed by two arching oaks. The way my jaw dropped at the sight of the hydrangea bushes in the front yard surprised even me; I'm not a green thumb, but something about their spring-time charm convinced me in a moment that I could be. Brick pavers encouraged us toward the door, and the fireplace in the living room made us look at each other with goofy grins. It was perfect.

Austin and I had been on the house hunt for just over a month. We had seen shiny new builds that lacked personality

[1] Michael Reeves, *Delighting in the Trinity: An Introduction to the Christian Faith* (Downers Grove, IL: IVP Academic, 2012), 62.

and '70s fixers with a tad too much. But this little home—the white brick ranch with the hydrangea bushes—felt like coming home.

It wasn't long before Austin and I were under contract on the home. As dreamy first-time buyers, we spent our weekends picking out paint swatches and imagining where all our apartment furniture and thrift store buys would look best. It was just a matter of time, it seemed, before this space would be our own—just a matter of waiting until we had the keys in hand.

We ticked along through the process so seamlessly that when the inspection report came back nine pages long, I hardly knew to give it another thought. Austin carried it into the living room one evening, and I could tell by the way his eyes fixated on the page that it was not the report he was expecting. Breaking from the page, his eyes met mine. "There's wood rot in the foundation," he sighed.

I searched his eyes for hints of what to make of the news. I knew it didn't sound good, but . . . was it really *that* bad? I shrugged my shoulders and gave him a blank stare. "So?"

My eyes widened as Austin read the report aloud. A sinking dining room. A tottering porch. A sag in the roof. A crack in that charming little fireplace. And each of them pointing back to the source of their misalignment: wood rot in the foundation.

It was a matter of hours before our contract on the home was terminated. Because the undergirding foundation was faulty, everything was amiss. Damage in those unseen, underlying supports showed up in more places than we could name and affected more than we imagined (or could afford to fix). That soggy, sinking foundation was just the beginning of the damage—damage that spread throughout the home like the roots of the oaks that ruled the front lawn.

Even to this day, I can call to mind all the beautiful things the home had to offer—that fireplace and crown molding, the brick pavers and front door. Each of them genuinely lovely, good, and beautiful; and each of them deeply affected by the underlying, unseen rot creeping beneath the surface.

The Church's One Foundation

There is no doctrine more uniquely Christian than the doctrine of the trinity. Both throughout church history and today, it is the Christian belief in a three-in-one God that sets us apart from all other faith systems. We are the only world religion to insist that God is not just one and not just plural, but *both*. Our God is a Trinitarian God.

And even while we know this, many of us (myself included) tend to approach the triune nature of God with an internal shrug of our shoulders. It's not that we believe the doctrine of the trinity is unimportant, we just aren't sure that it meets us on a discipleship level, and we can't articulate what difference it really makes in our daily walk with God. We look at it much like I looked at the inspection report; how much of a difference could this *really* make, we wonder. After all, there are more fun doctrines to get on to . . . like the doctrines of grace, the gospel, and Christology (the study of Christ).

But the Trinity is the theological foundation that undergirds the entire Christian faith. It is the doctrinal infrastructure on which our entire theological framework is built. Theologian Michael Horton put it this way: "The doctrine of the Trinity—God as one in essence and three in person—shapes and structures the Christian faith and practice in every way."[2] Fred Sanders echoes this sentiment: "Forget the Trinity and you forget why we do what we do; you forget who we are as gospel Christians."[3]

The doctrine of the trinity is not a theological appendage that we can take or leave without consequences. It is not an isolated theological construct, but at the very center of what it means to be Christian. Damage our doctrine of the trinity and you lose everything in tow. Our gospel sags. Our Christology

---

[2] Michael Horton, *Pilgrim Theology: Core Doctrines for Christian Disciples* (Grand Rapids: Zondervan, 2011), 89.

[3] Fred Sanders, *The Deep Things of God: How the Trinity Changes Everything* (Second Edition) (Wheaton, IL: Crossway, 2017), 9.

slopes. Put a crack in the Christian foundation of the trinity and you damage everything we know and love of grace.

But (here's the best news), set aright, our Trinitarian theology is the sure and stable structure that underpins everything else. When our doctrine of God mirrors the three-in-one nature proclaimed throughout Scripture, it *also* shows up in more places than we can name. Lay a firm foundation of Trinitarian doctrine and you'll find grace immovable, unwavering, and fixed. You'll find the gospel steady and secure. You'll notice your Christology is properly rooted and rightly braced.

When the doctrine of the trinity is properly fixed in place, you'll find yourself—warmly and wonderfully—theologically at home.

God Triune

For many of us, our first thoughts about God begin in Genesis 1:1. At the dawn of time and on the cusp of creation, we meet the God of the Bible for the first time. (Elohim, as the Hebrew Bible refers to him.) And you and I rightly revel in his creative power as he speaks the world into existence. We marvel as he crafts man from dust and breathes his life into those made in his image. We worship as his authority and power radiates throughout the opening chapters of Scripture.

But what was God doing before that? Before he created, before he breathed life, before he walked with man and woman in the garden . . . who was he? And, what was he doing? Who is the God of eternity past?

Jesus answers our question of what God was doing before anything else existed. He says, "Father . . . you loved me before the creation of the world" (John 17:24 NIV). Before there was a blade of grass or a ray of sunshine, God was a Father loving his Son and sending forth his Spirit. Into eternity past, God was happily, perfectly, contentedly triune.

The reality of the Trinity means that God is both three and one. There is one God who—from eternity past and into eternity future—exists as three distinct persons: Father, Son, and Holy Spirit. The common language that believers have honed throughout church history is this: God is one in essence and three in person.

This means that God is truly one (which is why Christianity falls rightly under mono-theism, the category of belief systems believing in one true God). This one God is proclaimed throughout Scripture. The Hebrew *Shema*—a declaration of worship that the people of God passed from generation to generation—insists, "Hear, O Israel: The LORD our God, the LORD is *one*" (Deut. 6:4–5, emphasis mine). The prophets repeat this reminder to God's people: "This is what the LORD says . . . I am the first and I am the last, apart from me there is no God" (Isa. 44:6 NIV). And the New Testament echoes this ancient truth: "Yet for us there is *one* God" (1 Cor. 8:6, emphasis mine).

And yet, the Bible also teaches us that God is three distinct persons: Father, Son, and Spirit. The Scriptures are emphatic about this: The Father is God (Phil. 1:2), the Son is God (Col. 1:19), and the Spirit is God (2 Cor. 3:17). God really is three—the Son is not the Father, the Father is not the Spirit, and the Spirit is not the Son. The three persons of the Godhead are distinct from each other, do defined tasks, and have unique roles in the plan of redemption. The Father sends the Son (1 John 4:14), the Son dwelt among us in the flesh (John 1:14) in order to become the sacrifice for our sins, and the Spirit bears witness to the Son (John 15:26).

Who God Is Not

The God of the Bible is truly triune—precisely three in one. And it's hard to wrap our minds around this mystery. It's baffling and stretching as we try to comprehend how two seemingly contradictory things can gloriously coexist in our God. We wrack our brains to know what to say about this God because the concept is so far beyond us.

It's in moments like these that I'm grateful for the relief of other theologians who feel like I feel, and maybe you feel, as we bump against this holy mystery. Michael F. Bird writes,

> It is generally easier and less problematic to say what the Trinity is not—not one God with three faces, not three Gods, not a hierarchy consisting of one big God with a supreme angel and divine power—than to say what the Trinity actually is.[4]

And he's right. The complexity of the concept often makes it easier to speak of who God is not, rather than who he is. Because we are humans with limited minds, when we work hard to articulate who God is with precision, our limited natures produce something of a theological mess. Our efforts to nail down the nature of the Trinity are akin to a nine-year-old pinning insects on a poster-board for the science fair: we have to kill the object of our study to do so. In our attempts to detail God's infinite nature with finite minds and vocabulary, we're bound to botch the threeness or the oneness of the Trinity.

And so we must also say who God is *not*. God is not like an egg: three parts of one whole. God is not really one person with three roles, as I am an individual person who is a sister, wife, and daughter. God is not one divine being with the ability to appear in three different forms, like water is one element that can appear in liquid, solid, and gas forms.

I remember the first time I read the Athanasian Creed in seminary and chuckled to myself (aloud in a quiet library, I might add). I wasn't raised in a church tradition that read or recited the

---

[4] Michael F. Bird, *What Christians Ought to Believe: An Introduction to Christian Doctrine through the Apostles' Creed* (Grand Rapids: Zondervan, 2016), 60.

creeds, and so I found myself reading one of the more historic creeds at twenty-four years old in the silent Gordon-Conwell library. The section on the Trinity is lengthy for the very reasons we just discussed: it's hard to say what God is like without also clarifying what he is not like.

> The Father eternal, the Son eternal, and the Holy Spirit eternal. And yet they are not three eternals, but one Eternal.
>
> As also there are not three incomprehensibles, nor three uncreated, but one Uncreated, and one Incomprehensible. So likewise the Father is Almighty, the Son Almighty, and the Holy Spirit Almighty. And yet they are not three almighties, but one Almighty.
>
> So the Father is God, the Son is God, and the Holy Spirit is God. And yet they are not three gods, but one God.
>
> So likewise the Father is Lord, the Son Lord, and the Holy Spirit Lord. And yet not three lords, but one Lord.[5]

We feel your pain, Athanasius.

At some point, all the analogies we use to talk about the Trinity simply fall short. And that's because our triune God is so far beyond us—gloriously, wondrously beyond us. This reminds us that we worship a God who has not been made by human hands or intellect. It also reminds us that we owe a great debt of gratitude to those throughout church history who have worked to say what we can about the Trinity, without saying more than we can: God is one in essence and three in person.

God is truly one, and truly three. He is triune.

---

[5] *The Athanasian Creed*, http://www.reformedspokane.org/Doctrine_pages/Christian%20Doctrine%20pages/Eccumenical%20Creeds/Athanasian%20Creed.html.

God before Time

The difficulty of wrapping our minds around the concept of the Trinity raises the question: Does all of this really matter? With how much we labor to speak rightly of the triune God of eternity past, wouldn't it just be easier to start with the God of Genesis 1:1? Why can't we, as Christians, just start with a Creator-God and go from there?

The reason is revealed in Christ's garden prayer: love.

That God was loving his Son and sending forth his Spirit from eternity past results in an entirely different kind of God than we would otherwise have. A fundamentally Creator-God would only learn to love once he had created something to love, something to express affection and delight. A God that is not Trinitarian before creation—a singular or solo God—does not know love in and of himself. Affection would be foreign to him; it must be learned, it must be created.

But a Trinitarian God is entirely different. Stretching into eternity past, God has been loving. How do we know? Because before creation, he loved his Son. Between the Father, Son, and Spirit existed a perfect love encapsulated in their three-in-one nature. He did not need to create something in order to love; he did not need to learn how to love. He was love, expressed love, and was loved all before the foundations of creation. This means, friend, he did not make you as some sort of experiment, or because he was lonely and required a companion in his eternal existence. He made you not out of need for love, but out of something else, something unexpected, something awe-inspiring.

Eternal Contentment, Eternal Community

I remember well the first summer I lived alone. I had just graduated from college and took a nanny position that would allow me to stay in downtown Chicago (arguably the best city in the world . . . at least during the summer months). At twenty-two years old, I was excited about the adventures the summer would bring. And after two years as an RA, I was craving the alone time that solo city living would afford me. I had a vision of making great meals and taking long walks along the lake; I imagined myself riding my bike and enjoying contented evenings at home sipping tea.

But my expectations were not my reality. I was alone a lot (I had gotten that part right), but it wasn't a satisfying aloneness. My introverted-self recovered from being an RA in about a week, which left me exactly eleven weeks of leaving an empty apartment for work, coming home to an empty space, and laying my head down on my pull-out couch at night with the pang of loneliness deep inside my gut.

God is so unlike us.

The love of the Trinity is the eternal experience of our triune God. It means that, before the dawn of time, God was perfectly complete and content in and of himself; God enjoyed the unrivaled, harmonious community of his own presence. He didn't need creation to give him community—he has that within himself. He didn't require mankind to bring him contentment—he has that within himself too.

Fred Sanders puts it this way: "In himself and without any reference to a created world or the plan of salvation, God is that being who exists as the triune love of the Father for the Son in the unity of the Spirit. The boundless life that God lives in himself, at home, within the happy land of the Trinity above all worlds, is perfect. It is complete, inexhaustibly full, and infinitely blessed."[6]

Unlike my post-grad self, God has always been at home with himself. He has never been uneasy or isolated. He has no personal vacancies that beg created beings come and fill. "Creation was not required," Sanders reminds us, "not mandatory, not exacted

---

[6] Sanders, *The Deep Things of God*, 62.

from God, neither by any necessity imposed from outside nor by any deficit lurking within the life of God."[7]

Within the community of himself, the Father, Son, and Spirit take perfect delight. They are wildly happy and at ease. In the "happy land of the Trinity," God enjoys his own company without the uneasy pangs of loneliness.

And this does not diminish the joy of God's creative activity; instead, it enhances it! Earlier I told you God created you (and everything else) out of something unexpected, something awe-inspiring. And here it is: God did not create out of need but out of *delight*. Rather than making something to satisfy himself, God creates out of the love and satisfaction of his own nature. In his mighty act of creative power, God expresses the love he has always possessed within himself to his creation, and welcomes us into the love he has known for all eternity.

So often when we talk about the Trinity, we look for hints of it on the pages of the creation narrative. Surely it is the "let us" of Genesis 1:26 that whispers the Trinitarian reality of God's nature, but it is his determination to make mankind in his image that warms us through with the realization that we were made in the image of this triune God. In speaking "us" on the sixth day of creation, the triune God gave us more than an inkling of his existence; *he gave us his very image*. We were created in love to love; created in community to commune; created in God's own satisfaction to find our ultimate satisfaction in him.

Not a Messenger

It is community that teaches us to communicate, which is why our early years of childhood are so formative for us. We've all heard the heart-breaking stories of abandoned children who grew up without the affection of community. The result in maturity is unmistakable: they have no idea how to communicate.

---

[7] Ibid., 65.

In many of the most horrific stories, children can reach their adolescent years without learning how to speak. Why? Because they didn't grow up in community, communication is not in their nature.

Imagine, again, a non-triune (or a solo) god in eternity past. What is he like? He cannot be relational, to say the least. And he cannot be affectionate, for how can any kind of affection for another grow in such eternal isolation? And when this god creates, how would he know how to relate to his creatures? It wouldn't be in love, and it might not be at all. After all, it's not in his nature to communicate because he does not come from community.

Let's say, for the sake of argument, that this god does want to communicate with his creation. How would he do it? He may consider sending a proxy—someone to represent him to his creation. He may send a message of sorts—some kind of letter that explains who he is. But that is the very best a singular god of isolation can do.

But the opposite is true of the triune God. From eternity past, God has been a relational God because he is triune. He is a communicating God precisely because he is triune.

In other words, because God is Trinity, he is the Word.

You see it is the glory of the Trinity that leads us directly to the foot of the manger, where God was made flesh to be the Word of God in human form for us. Jesus embodied the message of heaven to his fallen, estranged creation. When God wanted his creation to know exactly who he is, what he is like, and to make a way for them to be in right relationship with him again, he himself came to earth—not just to speak a word about God, but to *be* the Word of God for his people.

It's God's three-in-one communing nature that fundamentally leads him to express himself to the world, fuels in him a desire to be known by his creation, and wells within him the grace to bridge the communication gap between his divine self and his fallen, loved creatures. Because community is fundamentally who he is as the triune God, he delights in making himself known to his people. And God doesn't send a proxy or a messenger; he doesn't send a letter. He comes himself to make himself known in the community of his creation.

The Trinity, a Grace

Grace is a word whose meaning is easy to forget. It has been used so frequently (and sometimes, so flippantly) that we miss its unique definition: grace is the free, undeserved gift of God.

Grace is more than mercy. Mercy is God not giving me the punishment my sins require. But grace goes a step further—grace gives me more than pardon; grace loads my arms up with unmerited favor and sends me home with more gifts than I can fit in my car.

Grace is lavish and undeserved.

John, when keeping a gospel account of the work of Christ, sets out to remind us that when Christ was made flesh as the Word of God, he came to do one thing: to bring the reality of heaven to bear in the world.

> In the beginning was the Word [Jesus]. . . . And the Word became flesh and dwelt among us, and we have seen his glory, glory as of the only Son from the Father, full of grace and truth. . . . For from his fullness we have all received, grace upon grace. . . . No one has ever seen God; the only God, who is at the Father's side, he has made him known. (John 1:1, 14–16, 18)

The Son, who eternally shared the glory of the Father, became flesh and lived among humankind so that he might spill out onto the earth the fullness of heaven. When the triune God desired to express his very nature to the world, he himself came to earth. And what word does John use to describe what has been communicated? When God's eternal nature cracked open and poured out onto earth in Christ, what did we receive?

Not just grace. But grace upon grace.

Christ shared with you and I the fullness of the glory that the Father and Son have shared eternally. And when God's nature was revealed to his rebellious creatures, he wasn't unveiled as an eternally disappointed God or a divinely loathsome Ruler. Christ made the Father known, and *from his fullness we have received grace upon grace.*

A Trinitarian Gospel

Because God is Trinity in eternity past, fundamental to his nature is not what he has done (as it would be with a Creator-God), but who he is: he is a Father loving his Son in the unity and fellowship of his Spirit. And his Fatherly nature isn't restricted to the creation account (after all, wise parents will tell you that the task of fatherhood does not end at creation) but continues onto every page of Scripture.

Reeves sheds light: "It is not that this God 'does' being Father as a day job, only to kick back in the evenings as plain old 'God.' It is not that he has a nice blob of fatherly icing on top. He is Father. All the way down. Thus all that he does he does as Father. That is who he is."[8]

Because God is Father "all the way down," he is the God the rest of the Scriptures proclaim. Throughout the Old Testament, his people call him "Father" (Deut. 32:6; Isa. 63:16; Jer. 3:4), and he rescues and defends Israel, whom he names his "firstborn" (Exod. 4:22–23). When they are weak and unable, God carries his people "as a father carries his son" (Deut. 1:31 NIV). Like a good father, he disciplines his children (Deut. 8:5), has compassion on them (Ps. 103:13), and he loves them and teaches them to walk (Hosea 11:1–4).

---

[8] Reeves, *Delighting in the Trinity*, 23.

And when they fall into sin—breaking from his likeness and straying from his good desires for their safety and holiness—he saves them as only a Father can: into sonship.

A non-Trinitarian God not only lacks love, but lacks the warmth of the gospel narrative. Imagine with me, just for a moment, that instead of a Father-God we know a Ruler-God in eternity past. What kind of God is he? We already know he cannot create in love, for what would he know of love? And if he does create (having no good reason to), his creation cannot be more than minions for his charge. With this Ruler-God, what is the Fall but merely rebellion against his authority? What is salvation but merely being brought back under his loveless rule, perhaps to be pardoned from banishment in his dominion?

God is Ruler of the universe, yes. And the Fall does include rebellion against his authority. But a Fatherly God is entirely different from one who is a Ruler *alone*, and the narrative of the Scriptures bends to his Trinitarian nature. He creates in love and gives life in delight because that is essentially what a Father is. That is what it means to be a Father. It is the nature of a Father to beget children, to impart to them his image, and to nurture them in parental care. With a Fatherly God, what is the Fall but rebellion against a loving father and a resulting broken relationship? And what is salvation but a restoration to family unity, brought into right relationship with him as sons and daughters of God?

You see, the gospel insists that we are not only pardoned for our sins by God, but that through Christ we are made to be sons and daughters of our eternal Father. Through faith in Christ, God the Spirit unites us to God the Son, and God the Father receives us as his very own children. When God saves us, he does more than simply bring us back under his rule; he welcomes us into the love and fellowship of the eternal Trinity.

The Trinity, Our Sanctification

As redeemed sons and daughters of God, he has not just adopted us legally and left us without a new way of living. Instead, God brings us into his family and nurtures us in his likeness. The theological term for the process by which God makes us more like him is called *sanctification*. While salvation is the gift of God that secures our place in God's family for eternity, sanctification is the ongoing work he does in our hearts and lives by his Spirit (1 Cor. 6:11).

And how does God do this? How does God make us more like himself? By fixing our eyes on Christ. In all the places where the Fall has bent us inward, the sanctifying work of the Spirit is to bend our stubborn necks back that we might gaze on the Lord of our salvation. Where our inborn sin left us selfish and self-protecting, it's the ongoing work of the Spirit of God that lifts our heads and sets our eyes on Christ in whose image we were made and are being remade. Yes, if you are a Christian today, that's God's purpose for your life: to remake you into the image of his Son.

And it's all too fitting that this is the work of the Spirit. God the Spirit sets our eyes on Jesus because that is where his eyes have eternally been. The persons of the Godhead have each eternally been outward-looking, eyes fixed on the other holy persons: the Father is eternally pouring out his affection on the Son, in the love-bond and fellowship of the Spirit. The Son is always glorifying the Father. And the Spirit is always making much of the Son. As God welcomes us into right relationship through salvation, he welcomes us into this privilege: to set our eyes on Christ, the glorious landscape of his gaze for all of eternity.

Help for the Unloving

And just when we feel too undeserving for this kind of intimate Fatherly relationship with the triune God, our hearts overwhelmed by our own inability to respond to God with the same level of love that he has lavished on us, we read the reassuring prayer of the second person of the Trinity, Jesus:

> *O righteous Father, even though the world does not know you, I know you, and these know that you have sent me. I made known to them your name, and I will continue to make it known, **that the love with which you have loved me may be in them**, and I in them. (John 17:25–26, emphasis mine)*

Do you worry that you will not love the Father to the level you should? Do you feel discouraged at the state of your own sanctification, wondering how you could have responded so unlovingly to the eternally loving triune God? Does your response to this doctrine strike you as surprisingly cool or indifferent? Christ's own prayer to the Father is a burden-lifting promise for us: he will fill us with the love the Father has for the Son. By the help of the Spirit and by our union with Christ, we have unrelenting aid in loving the Father back, in delighting in his nature, and in fixing our eyes on him.

Or perhaps you worry that God could not love you as much as he loves other Christians. Surely you've done too much (or too little) to warrant his affection. Your faults and failures leave you with a burdening question: *How much could God really love me?* You can answer your own question in how you respond to this one: How much do you think the Father loves his Son? How big, how wide, how deep is that love? As we are found in Christ, the affectionate eyes of the Father are fitted on us in love and affection beyond our wildest imaginations.

A Lookout Point

I still remember where I was sitting when Austin asked me to hike my first 14er (a mountain exceeding 14,000 feet). We were living in Colorado and I was sitting at our dining room table in our little apartment that overlooked the foothills (to be perfectly honest, out the window was how I preferred to see the mountains most of the time). Austin had found a peak just outside of Breckenridge that he wanted to climb, and he wanted us to do it together. While on vacation.

With much encouragement and reassurance, I agreed to the hike. And later that fall while on our anniversary getaway, at 5:15 a.m. we found ourselves packed and ready to climb Mount Quandary in the beautiful mountains of southwest Colorado.

We started making our way along the trail through the trees in the dark, with only our headlamps for light. We had to step carefully over rocks and around fallen trees, working to plant our feet solidly in the dark. When we broke through the tree line and the sun started to rise, I ignorantly asked, "Does this mean the dicey part is behind us?" Austin slowly turned toward me with a look of concern. His expression held my answer: it most certainly was not.

What I didn't realize (or bother to research beforehand) is that Quandary is known for a ridge that leads to the peak. You climb quickly in elevation for a while before a ridge stretches out before you like a sling-back with steep slopes on either side. On that last push of the hike, you have be extra cautious, choosing your steps with care and ensuring that you don't put too much weight on any single rock to the right or to the left. To get to the top of the peak, you must find your feet at the center of trail, letting care lead to confident foot-placement.

The conversation about the Trinity can feel this way. Knowing our human limitations, we are rightly cautious not to say too much or too little about God's triune nature. We mark out the historic language for the Trinity, ensuring that we don't inadvertently wander into heretical language and descriptions.

Indeed, we must be careful. But when we find our feet at the center of that path—when we are disciplined in our language and studied in our descriptions—we find that what opens up for us is the glory of the redemption story. And when that happens, it's not long before all we've learned makes its way into our very worship habits: each time we seek contentment in God alone, for example, we practice a willful recognition of God's eternal self-satisfaction. When we praise him for his lavish love, we praise him for his triune nature. As we savor and study the Word of God in our personal quiet times or corporately in our churches, we worship him as a communicating, triune God. And as we receive the gentle unbending of the Spirit—yielding our will to his way and letting him fix our eyes on Christ—we rightly submit to the God who is Trinity.

Austin and I did eventually make it to the top of Quandary, and I can say unequivocally that it was worth it. Every step and water break and moment spent wondering if my legs would ever stop shaking was worth it because we reached the top. And there, we saw why so many found their feet on that path. It was breathtakingly beautiful.

We walk the center of the theological path as we talk about the Trinity, not for fear of falling so much as anticipation of the joy ahead. What lies on the other side of proper thinking about God is breathtakingly worshipful. And just when we wonder if all the fuss is worth it, if it really makes a difference to know God as Trinity rather than only as Creator or Ruler, we get a glimpse of God's glorious, beautiful nature and know: yes. Unequivocally, it is worth it.

Getting a glimpse of God's Trinitarian nature will make you crawl up theological banks and scrape your knees in study just to learn more about what you're looking at. When we think on God and dwell on his triune nature, we can't help but hunger to explore the Word for lookout points of his divinity and displays of his three-in-one nature. The Trinity isn't a side point or a byline in our theological statement—something that we believe but do so without affection or joy. The Trinity is our God. It is everything about him. It is the very substance of the gospel. It is the content of grace. And because God was Trinity at the very beginning of time, we can have confidence: he is the same on every page of Scripture, who will bring us home in the end.

Christology: Worshiping God Incarnate

He [God] took pity on them, therefore, and
did not leave them destitute in the knowledge
of Himself, lest their very existence should
prove purposeless. For of what use is existence
to the creature if it cannot know its Maker?[1]
St. Athanasius

I crane my neck to the right, letting the tendons strain against my desire to stretch them. I tilt to the right and feel the same. The familiar pain of sciatic tingling—undoubtedly caused by my habitual impatience at the gym—runs from my right hip, behind my knee, and down the outside of my calf muscle. I can feel my right shoulder tightening; there's a muscle knot that likes to form behind my shoulder blade whenever too much of any day is given to typing.

---

[1] St. Athanasius of Alexandra, *St. Athanasius on the Incarnation: The Treatise De Incarnatione Verbi Dei.* Translated and Edited by a Religious of C.S.M.V. (London: A. R. Mowbray & Co., 1953).

I shift in my seat, hoping it will help. It does not. I, and my uncomfortable body, am still right here, confined to this office chair where I will work until my work is done (or until 5 p.m. arrives with relief).

In moments like these I am keenly aware that I am embodied. There is no way for me to do my work, complete my tasks, occupy my office apart from my body. Together with my immaterial soul, this material flesh and blood—muscles that pull and age and, at times, spasm—is always with me, and is, in fact, *me*. Where this body is, is where I am in my entirety.

I—my whole self—am right here.

This is a reality we all come to know at some point or another. In fact, the reality that we can only be in one place at one time is a comfort to us in many ways. Existentially, it's convenient that we can't be in more places than one at a time because otherwise we would be expected to be. We'd have to pick up from soccer and ballet . . . at the same time. We'd have to be at our office desk and prepping dinner simultaneously. But because we're located in one place at one time, our human limitations (though frustrating at times) offer our already hectic schedules a sigh of relief.

But more than that, it's our human limitation to be exclusively in one place at a time that gives meaning to our physical presence. It's why time over coffee with a friend, a business deal made in the same conference room between two partners, and a visitor who steps inside your hospital room mean so much— because we can only be one place at a time, and we chose to be in that place, with those people. It's the gentle squeeze of our spouse's hand while we sit in the doctor's office waiting room that reminds us that they're in it with us. It's why when a child wakes from a nightmare in the dark of 2 a.m., her father's words are more soothing than flipping the light switch: "I'm right here."

The Gap between God and Man

When we consider the glorious mystery of God triune, we feel the gap between ourselves and our God. We work and study and underline and highlight and reread in efforts to wrap our minds around our three-in-one God. We worship God as Father, Son, and Spirit, and simultaneously as the one true God in whom there is no separation. And as we settle into the wonder and mystery of the Trinity, we are well aware of two distinct realities: God is greater than us, and we are not God.

Of all the doctrines I can name, there are few that so painfully highlight for me our human separation from God. We are not him and we are not like him. He is desperately beyond us, beyond our conception, and beyond our existence. We peer into the wonder of God's nature on every page of Scripture, and, as we do, we say with Paul:

> *Oh, the depth of the riches and wisdom and knowledge of God! How unsearchable are his judgments and how inscrutable his ways! (Rom. 11:33)*

The gap between God's nature and our own is great. And in our human limitations, there was nothing that we could do about it. We couldn't ascend to heaven and be like him (humanity tried that once, and it did not go as planned; ask the builders of Babel), nor could we elevate our human minds to even conceive of his nature. At various times and in various ways he revealed himself—through creation and prophets and such—but our minds were too darkened to understand (Heb. 1:1–2; Rom. 1:21). No, we could not go to him or be like him or even understand what he had shared about himself. If we were ever to fully know him, he would have to come to us. He would have to become like us.

The glory of the doctrine of the incarnation is this: he did.

God, in his eternal desire to be known by his creation whom he loves, condescended to us in human form that we might know him. Though we could not become like him, he became like us in the God-Man Jesus Christ that the Father might be revealed to us, known by us, and worshiped by us. He came in the only form we understood—flesh, blood, ligaments, and bone—that we might see God and know him.

Not Less Than God, Not More Than Human

The incarnation—the theological word we use to reference the historic reality that the Son of God became man—is God's way of generously revealing himself to us (often called God's *self-revelation*). Because it is in his nature to relate to his creation in love, he didn't send a proxy or a messenger to communicate his divine nature to the limited minds of his creation. No, he came *himself* to not only reveal himself, but to bring us to himself.

This is why it is so eternally beautiful and theologically vital that we understand the nature of the incarnation: that the Son of God became wholly man without ceasing to be wholly God. In the person of Jesus Christ, God's full divine nature and the very essence of what it means to be human meet so thoroughly that his dual natures cannot be separated. Christ cannot be dissected into his God-nature and human-nature because he is *fully* God and *fully* man. In more blunt and unromantic terms, his divine to human ratio is not 50/50, but 100/100. His human nature did not diminish his divine glory, nor was his human nature a faux finish on his divine being. The mystery and joy of the incarnation is that the second person of the Trinity became fully man without ceasing to simultaneously be fully God.

At this point, you might be wondering: *What is the point of all these "simultaneous" natures of God?* It's hard for our minds to hold these two realities together—God is three *and* one? Christ is God *and* man? But if the mission of God was to make himself known to his creation, and if the way we could comprehend him is in our own human form, then it is imperative that the Incarnated One be both fully God and fully man. God didn't want to just give his creation an ounce of his nature, like an appetizer to wet our taste while keeping the real divine entrée in heaven. He desired to reveal his eternal, divine nature to his people—himself, as he truly is! Someone with one ounce of divinity would not do the job of revealing who God actually is, for God certainly has more than one ounce. So with every ounce of divinity in tow, he came in the form that we could best understand—in our very form, a body just like ours that we might truly know him.

Access to Knowledge of God

When my and Austin's house hunt came to an end, we were relieved. After seeing over thirty-five houses, going through multiple inspections, and negotiating mind numbing details with the seller, we finally found ourselves sitting in a law office preparing for closing. It was glorious.

Until it wasn't. See, Austin and I are planners. We love to prepare and have all our ducks in a row. And we thought we did . . . until it came time to produce our down payment method. Austin and I had missed one very important logistical instruction in the closing process: all down payments must be made with certified funds.

Certified funds are a payment method that banks use to guarantee a payment. Certified checks are written by a bank at the request of the account holder, and they carry the value of the little number typed in the "amount" line. This means that once your bank produces a certified check for you, you are holding the money in your hand, much like cash. Flush a personal check down the toilet and, oh well, you're just out the paper it cost to print the personal check. But do the same with the certified check for a down payment? Well, you just lost your long-earned savings.

Certified checks carry the value of the payment so that there's no chance of the check bouncing; the recipient of the check is guaranteed to receive their due in full. And that's what the bank wanted at our closing, of course. We planners in the room were so embarrassed by the fact that we only brought with us a personal checkbook (and the way the lawyer kept telling us that it happens all the time with first-time home buyers only made us feel worse).

In hindsight, the remedy was simple: we called the bank, they issued the funds, the law office received their payment in a matter of minutes, and the home was ours (or, at least 20 percent of it was). And what made all the difference? What put the home title in our name? Certified funds.

It's paramount to our theology of the incarnation to know that God was fully man and fully God. Why? Because in the incarnation, God sent the entire value of his person—his entire nature, divine power, and eternal glory—to become man and live among us. This is why John writes this so poignantly for us in John 1:14:

> And the Word became flesh and dwelt among us,
> and **we have seen his glory**, glory as of the only Son
> from the Father, full of grace and truth. (emphasis
> mine)

The Son of God was made man in such a way that the entire value of the Godhead, the very nature of God's divine being, and the entire glory of the Father was manifested in human flesh. Christ carried the very value of God to the earth—losing none of his divine nature, soiling none of his holiness, and sacrificing not an ounce of his divinity. Just as when you hold cash or a certified check, you are holding the money *itself*—all of it—not something that merely promises it or points to it, so it is with Jesus. With the incarnated Christ, we are not looking at someone who merely promises God or points to God. We are looking at God *himself*—all of him, every ounce represented—in human form.

Because of this reality, when we wonder if we can know the Father, we can look to Christ and be assured: yes! God is knowable to you and I through the person of Jesus Christ. Guaranteed.

There is no room for Christ's divinity to be voided, no chance of his God-nature being devalued. In the incarnation, Jesus Christ made all the riches of God's nature accessible to you and me as he became the long-awaited God-Man.

Presence Promised

In the incarnation, the limitless Son of God confined himself to the restraints of physical space and time so that we might know the Father and experience the limitless comforts and joys of his presence. Christ is "the radiance of God's glory and the exact representation of [God's] being" (Heb. 1:3 NIV), which means that when we come near to Christ we are brought near to the Father. Our eternal Savior became as we are: limited to being in one place at one time, and in doing so, whispering the promise of God's presence among his people. Where is God? In Christ, he is right here.

When the darkness of our human frailty and fallenness reminds us of our inability to know God, when our sin and shame have overtaken us and our hope is as dark as night, when our fears and failures drown us in sorrow and God feels far from us, we can, because of Christ, call to the Father like a child waking in the night. We call out because we know we need more than a light switch; we need the Father himself to come and be our aid in the dark. We need his very presence.

In Jesus we know the rush of the loving Father to our side as his incarnated Son assures us, "I am right here." The fullness of God's glory and the entirety of God's presence, here. With us. For us. Bringing us salvation.

Access to God

Though we can know things about God through his creation, and though God revealed himself in various ways to people before the coming of Christ, the Bible says that his incarnation is the fullest and final access point to knowing him. Because we are limited by our human understanding, created form, and fallen nature, we cannot know God in our own efforts. But our triune God has made himself fully known to us in Jesus. This means that if the doctrine of the trinity is the foundation on which our theological house is built, the doctrine of the incarnation is the front door to that home. It's the incarnation—the very physical body of Jesus—that gives us access to the knowledge of God because it is the ultimate location of God's self-revelation to the world.

When Austin and I completed the real estate closing process at the law office, we were both a bit caught aghast when they handed us the keys. It was strange, on the one hand, to have paid so much money, gone through so much paperwork, and jumped through so many hoops to simply be handed two little pieces of strangely shaped metal. But that's not what caught us off guard. What took us aback is that we realized the unseen weight of those two ounces of silver: the home was ours. Not just the front door that held the matching keyhole, but the entire house. Every room, every cabinet, every light switch and toilet—ours. Because we had the keys in hand, we had access to the very heart of the home.

Jesus Christ became man so that we could know God. He himself—his physical body that resembles our own—is the exact location of our access to the Father. But God was not content to just make a way for us to know him intellectually, but to know him personally. In the incarnation, God didn't just want to communicate to us what he is like in his nature, as if rattling off some data about his divine being. No, he wanted to gift to us intimate, personal knowledge of God through the person of Jesus Christ.

> Jesus did not come to dispense arcane, previously hidden factoids about God that we are to mentally appropriate. Rather, the Son of God came to share with us his knowledge of God his

Father. He came, in other words, to incorporate us into his *experiential, relational knowledge* of the Father through the Spirit, to share the intimacy that characterizes their knowing of one another.[2]

The incarnation is not just our intellectual or theological access point to God, *he is* our very access to God. Through the person of Jesus Christ, a way was opened to you and me to know God personally, relationally, and intimately, which is why John reiterates: "And this is eternal life, that they know you, the only true God, and Jesus Christ whom you have sent" (John 17:3). This is why Jesus presses from his own human lips: "I am the door. If anyone enters by me, he will be saved" (John 10:9). God did not just do all this that we might have information about him, but in Christ he delights in handing us the very keys, granting us access by his Son to the entirety of his glory.

And just when we think that his generous work of condescending to us was finished, we remember the point altogether. Not just access, not just entrance, not just admission; but a home. God is not giving us a tour through his nature, but inviting us to enter through Christ into right relationship with him as our loving Father. In Jesus, the incarnated Son of God, the invitation was opened to us to bend our knees before him as Lord and Savior, to love him with affection and worship, and to be loved by the eternal Father as members of his own household.

> *"If anyone loves me, he will keep my word, and my Father will love him, **and we will come to him and make our home with him**." (John 14:23, emphasis mine)*

---

[2] John C. Clark and Marcus Peter Johnson, *The Incarnation of God: The Mystery of the Gospel as the Foundation of Evangelical Theology* (Wheaton, IL: Crossway, 2015), 50.

The Ministry of Christ's Body

Early church history is littered with heresies (which it why it is also, gratefully, littered with counsels to set these heresies aright). But few are as intriguing to me as the gnostic movement. This heretical movement arose out of the belief that Christ could not be fully man because physical flesh, they believed, is inherently evil. As the assumption went in that day, everything spiritual is pure, but everything physical is dirty, especially the body. They looked at the human body and saw a grotesque mass of cravings and desires, and believed it to be a sort of prison from which the soul would one day be released. From this vantage point, God could never take on something as "dirty" as a physical body! God would have no dealings with "evil" like that. To line up their Christology with their assumptions about the body, the Son of God, Gnostics claimed, only *appeared* to be human, but didn't actually take on any of the filthy bits of our humanity— like skin, bone, hair, toenails, and armpits.

This heresy was marked as such at the First Counsel of Nicaea in AD 325, but it still looms large in our Western culture. Though we wouldn't call human flesh "evil," we aren't entirely comfortable with it and it makes us just a bit uneasy to think about our Savior having nose hair and body odor.

The primary place we see this in our own theology today is in the way we often speak of the gospel narrative. While we know that Christ is our only access to the Father, it's all too easy for us to disassociate the salvation Christ offers us from the incarnation. We don't often think of the body of Christ—his physical self in which he was born, died, rose again, and returned to heaven—as the location of our salvation and the means of our justification.

But for the righteous demands of the Law to be satisfied, a paradoxical requirement had to be met: a sin-wrecked humanity owed a great debt to God that had to be paid by a sinless sacrifice. The physical hands that took the fruit from the forbidden tree in the garden, that rebelliously bit with their physical teeth and tongues, that looked down at their exposed physical bellies and breasts and genitals with eyes opened afresh, that spread through their physical offspring the fallenness of sin—these humans, *we humans*, needed a *human* Savior. And just not any human Savior, but One who could enter into the frailty of our physical form, remain sinless, and pay the bloody sacrifice for the sins we committed in our bodies.

And there was only One: the God-Man, Jesus Christ. Just as human as the hands that took the fruit and the hands that perpetuate sin today, so our Savior took on human form. He was born in flesh, carried in the womb by a teenage mother and brought into the world in the brokenness of a world without a room for him. He walked our earth, letting his once all-satisfied self grow hungry, letting his body ache with the pains of work and toil, reaching out his human hands to touch the infirm and the weak. In his body he died the excruciating death on the cross—an instrument devised by the evil hands of men for the torture of criminals and national enemies. And as he breathed a final breath in his human lungs, he surrendered himself to the darkness of human death—even death on a cross (Phil. 2:8).

Our human fallenness required an unblemished sacrifice to enter into the frail nature of our humanity. And so, in the abundance of his grace and mercy, "he made him to be sin who knew no sin, so that in him we might become the righteousness of God" (2 Cor. 5:21). All the way to the grave, all the way to the tomb, all the way to the death that God promised ages ago would be the destination at the end of the path of sin, Christ bore our humanity fully and finally.

And yet . . . our human grave could not hold him. Death could not keep him. After three days in the grave, breath returned to his human lungs. The blood vessels that had dried up in death were opened again as a rush of warm life flowed through his veins. His eyes opened. His feet hit the ground. And our Jesus, the incarnated Son of God, walked right out of the grave.

The Gnostics were wrong. The body isn't a dirty reality that our Savior kept himself neatly insulated from, but was the central instrument of our redemption as he entered fully into our humanity. Human flesh didn't soil his divinity, but his divinity penetrated the very center of our fallen humanity, breaking open the garden-old bondage to sin and the grave and making way for eternal life. It wasn't *apart* from human form, but *through* human form that God wrought our salvation—in the physical birth, physical death, and physical resurrection of Jesus Christ.

And while we might think that he would stop there—that the resurrection is the capstone of the redemptive narrative—he didn't. Though in the Fall human flesh was removed from the holy presence of God through banishment from the garden, God promised that he would one day make a way for mankind to be in right relationship with God again. God's way is Jesus. Jesus, in his resurrected body, ascended into heaven, into the presence of his Father, taking human flesh back into the presence of God again.

You see, God didn't just make a way for man to be right with him "on paper," as if justification is only a legal matter. God didn't just make a way for man to be with him ethereally, "as if" we were to be in his presence again. No, in the person of Jesus Christ, human flesh entered the very presence of God and holds out this hope of salvation to you and me: all who place their faith in this Incarnated One are united to him, join in his completed work and have the guarantee of eternal life in his likeness—in the very presence of the Father as sons.

The Ascended Christ

Austin and I are different kinds of movie-watchers—which makes Friday nights simultaneously fun and frustrating. Austin loves quality films; he sinks in deeply to the experience, and engages them thoroughly. Me? I'm all about the popcorn. I'm not as much there for the movie, as I am to ask questions throughout it. *Why does he have a gun? Why are they jamming that lock?*

Who's that guy in the jacket skulking in the background? It's quite annoying.

But for all the questions I ask during the movie, Austin's favorite (read: the *least* endearing question I ask) always comes at the end. *Is that how it really ends?* Even when wrapped up with a tidy little ending, my mind always goes beyond the closing scene. I wonder what the couple that finally got together will do about their ultimate differences as they build a life together; I wonder how long the recently rescued city will stay out of trouble; and I wonder how long the kingdom's happy ending could really last with other armies lurking around the bend. These questions always make Austin silently smile, while I sit there yammering about all the potential outcomes (undoubtedly with popcorn in my teeth).

Have you ever asked this question of the gospel narratives? Have you ever wondered about what happened after the closing scene? We are ready to forget that the Christ who was incarnated at the beginning of the book of John, lived and died and rose again throughout the book of John, and ascended to heaven at the end of the book of John is still incarnated today. In the presence of the Father, the Son of God remains in his resurrected, human flesh—taking his physical body into the presence of God for all of eternity. It means that in the incarnation, the second person of the Trinity became fully, irreversibly, and eternally enfleshed.

This reality gives substance to his ongoing ministry in the presence of the Father as he bridges the gap between man and God—not just in our knowledge of God, but in our representation before him. In his very person, Christ brings together the divide between the divine and the human as he intercedes on behalf of those who have placed their faith in him:

> *Who is to condemn? Christ Jesus is the one who died—more than that, who was raised—who is at the right hand of God, who indeed is interceding for us. (Rom. 8:34)*

The end of the Gospels is not the end of the incarnation story. It stretches out before us into eternity future. With joy, there will be a day when we will see our resurrected Savior face-to-face. As he is. In the flesh.

The Body of Christ, the Church

And we might wonder, at this point, what all that incarnation stuff means for the presence of God in this world. After all, one of the realities of human limitation is that we can only be in a single place at once. So, when Christ returned to heaven, did he take his divine presence with him?

The disciples wondered the same thing as they watched him return to his Father. And Jesus' reassuring words for them are a profound redefinition of our lives in Christ today:

> *"And I will ask the Father, and he will give you another advocate to help you and be with you forever—the Spirit of truth. . . . But you know him, for he lives with you and will be in you." (John 14:16–17 NIV)*

Where is the presence of God now? Yes, it's in heaven, but it's also still here on the earth, *indwelling all believers who place their faith in Christ.* The Holy Spirit, the third person of the Trinity, lives with and in all who come to God through the Incarnated One. Yes, the physical body of Christ ascended into heaven, but the presence of God has not left us. It is right here, in the church. God is present in the body of Christ.

Our human need for God's presence in the physical world is not new, but as old as the generations of people who walked with him. In the book of Exodus, God's people set up a Tent of Meeting for God to come and meet with Moses—and God did! He met with Moses, and he led his people with a pillar of fire by night and cloud by day. But one day, the pillar and the cloud appeared for the last time. Was God finished with his desire to be present with his people? No. God wasn't done. He then commanded his people to build him a tabernacle. The tabernacle was to be a place constructed for holy worship to a holy God, and God promised to meet with his people there. And as the people read their instructions to fashion poles to roll up and carry the tabernacle from place to place, they realized that embedded in the blueprints for the tabernacle plans were a reminder: this place of God's presence was also temporary.

And then there was the temple—the permanent home for God's dwelling! Or so God's people thought. But through their rebellion and wayward living, the temple was destroyed. God's home was in shambles. His home was among them no more.

The Tent of Meeting, the tabernacle, the temple—these places where God dwelt *among* men were always meant to point God's people forward to the One who would be Immanuel, God *with us* (Matt. 1:23). And as Christ ascended into heaven, he once again pronounced that something better was coming—the Holy Spirit. This would no longer be God merely among us, or even God with us, but God *in us*. Through the coming of the Spirit, the presence of God was cracked open and spilled out into the hearts of all those who call on the name of Jesus in faith. The body of Christ was redefined, expanded and stretched out across all tribes and tongues and peoples and language.

What a thought, right? Is it a thought you've had before? Has it ever struck you that your role as a member of the church, the body of Christ is to bear the presence of God in the world? It is a high calling, and one we are quick to neglect. In our fusses about local church politics and voting on the carpet color, we're much more prone to think of our roles in the church as housekeepers in the many houses of God. And that's if we take the call to be in a local church seriously at all.

But Jesus didn't call us his caretakers, housekeepers, or worker bees. Nor did he call us lone rangers. He called us his *body*. He says, "I am the light of the world. Whoever follows me will never walk in darkness but will have the light of life" (John 8:12 NIV);

and then in a pivot he tells his followers, "*You* are the light of the world" (Matt. 5:14, emphasis mine). How can this be except that Christ has really given us his Spirit, the Spirit of God himself, to dwell in and through us to bear the presence of God in his world?

This has far-reaching implications for life in the body of Christ, the church. Where we are prone to separate Christ's justifying work from his physical life, we are similarly prone to separating our life in Christ from life in his body. We are quick to think of salvation as "me and Jesus," and step aside from bothering with the messy stuff of church life.

But this is not what Christ offers us in salvation. He doesn't offer us salvation apart from his body, and he doesn't offer us salvation apart from the body. Or, put another way, there is no way to be saved into Christ without also being saved into his church. The church is his household, after all. Enter through Christ, and you find yourself gloriously at home in the Father's house along with every other believer who has entered in through that same incarnated access point. To be joined to Christ in faith is to become, by default, a member of his body on the earth.

This is why Paul doesn't abandon the fleshy language of the incarnation when speaking of the church today. Where he could talk about the church being a household, a family, or an assembly (all of which he does), his favorite language is bodily language.

> *That he worked in Christ when he raised him from the dead and seated him at his right hand in the heavenly places, far above all rule and authority and power and dominion, and above every name that is named, not only in this age but also in the one to come. And he put all things under his feet and gave him as head over all **things to the church**, **which is his body**, the fullness of him who fills all in all. (Eph. 1:20–23, emphasis mine)*

*From whom **the whole body, joined and held
together by every joint** with which it is equipped,
when each part is working properly, **makes the
body grow** so that it builds itself up in love. (Eph.
4:16, emphasis mine)*

*For just as **the body** is one and has many members,
and all the members of **the body**, though many, are
one body, so it is with Christ. For in one Spirit we
were all baptized into one body—Jews or Greeks,
slaves or free—and all were made to drink of one
Spirit.*

*For the body does not consist of one member but
of many. If **the foot** should say, "Because I am not **a
hand**, I do not belong to **the body**," that would not
make it any less a part of **the body**. And if **the ear**
should say, "Because I am not an eye, I do not belong
to **the body**," that would not make it any less a part
of **the body**. (1 Cor. 12:12–16, emphasis mine)*

We much prefer to be gnostic, don't we? We don't like the
messiness of human relationships, and we would often much
rather have Jesus on our own than meet him among his people.
But Paul doesn't indicate to us that there's any room for a me-
and-Jesus kind of salvation. Instead, he insists (as Christ does)
that all who enter through Christ join in the family of faith that
stretches out beyond national borders, beyond denominational
boundaries, beyond our own generation and the one to come.
God is present in this world through his body, through the
church, and therein lies our life in Christ.

Very Good to Very Good

As our culture grows more and more delighted in disem-
bodiment—through online "communities," through diets that

insist we take up less and less space in this world, and through technical advances that help us avoid human interactions when simply going to the grocery store—we as Christians have the distinct opportunity to embrace God's good gift of embodiment. Christians don't reject our physical bodies as evil. Why? Because of the incarnation.

The Christian witness regarding the human body spans the entire metanarrative of Scripture. It looks back to the garden and believes the pronouncement of God over the first human flesh: it is "very good" (Gen. 2). And though sin entered the world through human rebellion and passes our sinful nature from generation to generation, we believe the promise of God: one day, a Savior would come in our likeness to pay the penalty of our sin.

We believe that Christ became fully, physically human without losing an iota of his holiness and divinity. In his body, he was the ultimate sacrifice our sin required. And when he had completed this sacrificial work, he didn't shed his body for a "superior" existence; he rose bodily from the dead. The Father didn't finally "let" Jesus escape his body upon death, he *resurrected* it.

The hope we have in salvation—the promise of God for our very real human future—is not ascending out of our bodies some kind of ascetic existence where we enjoy a spiritual reality as a formless soul, but a promise of resurrection life. The Christian hope is that our *bodies* will be raised, just as Christ's was. We will be physically resurrected, renewed, and remade.

From Genesis to Revelation the Scriptures testify against our gnostic culture. The body is not an evil we hope to escape; human flesh is not something yucky that we hope to minimize. The body isn't the prison cell where our truer self, our soul, is trapped and awaiting liberation. Human flesh cannot be any of these things, because in the incarnation God ordained it that a human body, the body of his Son, is the lynchpin of our salvation as we worship the One who bodily died, bodily rose, and bodily ascended into heaven.

A Body of Suffering

I keep catching myself running ahead. I want to rush on to related theological topics like the church, the Holy Spirit, salvation, and final things. By this point, you can see how this doctrine of the incarnation spills easily over into a thousand other theological categories. It informs how we live in our homes, bodies, churches, and more. It shapes the way we approach the Lord's Supper—his body broken for us. It changes what we believe about and how we engage the physical world and God's ultimate plan for a resurrected humanity and a renewed creation.

But, while we could apply this doctrine in a thousand different places, I want to camp out on one for a moment. I believe that a vibrant theology of the incarnation has far-reaching ramifications for us in one particular arena and one that the Western church has long wrestled with: a theology of suffering.

We believe that Jesus died and rose again, but the way we conceive of it is often more theoretical than it is realistic. Think on this for a moment: our God became fully man (without ceasing to be fully God, of course). He felt the aches and pains of an aging body, bent his back under physical labor and the toil of working to sustain his own life and that of his family. When he laid on the hard ground while traveling, he felt rocks under his shoulders. Surely he endured more than one sleepless night in his ministry. He woke the next day, not to an extra cup of coffee, but with bags pulling at his lower lids. He was tired. He grew hungry. He was sore. He was embodied and experienced everything that having a body entails.

Christ made his way to the cross knowing that his death would be physically excruciating. A citizen of the city, he had likely passed by crucified corpses hanging on the hilltop or along the road. He saw the dusty remains of criminals and conspirators as the birds flocked over their decaying bodies. As he did, he knew what the future held: he knew he would go to the cross, endure agonizing physical pain, and would sink down into the darkness of death on our behalf.

I wonder if he ever paused on an ordinary Tuesday and let his fingers run over his hands, knowing they would very soon be pierced. I wonder if he ever felt the passing of chronological time inching ever toward that dark Good Friday and felt like cattle on a conveyor belt heading helplessly toward the slaughter. I wonder if he ever hit his head while working wood as a carpenter, felt a trickle of blood slip down through his hair, and paused to recall that one day a crown of thorns would sink their teeth in that same skin much more deeply.

Our incarnated God experienced unimaginable physical suffering on our behalf in order to bring us eternal life. He let his eyes close on the cross, let his lungs press their final, aching breath so that you and I could be brought into the eternal life that rightly belonged to him. And the Scriptures are clear: Christ did not despise this suffering, but took up with joy for the cross set before him (Heb. 12:1–2). The physical suffering he endured in his body was not something he abhorred, hated, or loathed. He did not sneer at the suffering he experienced in his incarnated body; he did not mock, revile, or disdain the path of suffering before him. He walked in it with joy, knowing that the suffering he bore in his body was giving glory to the Father and walking us into union with himself.

One of the greatest lies Christianity faces in our day is that bodily suffering evidences a lack of spiritual substance. This is the atrocious falsehood propagated by the prosperity gospel, teaching Christians that if their bodies break, bend, and are burdened, that something in their spiritual life is awry. The lie goes like this: God intends to make you healthy, wealthy, and wise—if only you could believe more, pray harder, and hope more diligently!

But, friends, as we are united to the incarnated Christ, why should we expect our lives to look so drastically different from his own? Are we not included in the suffering of Christ? Is not the ministry of the gospel one of also taking up our crosses? Is not the hope Christ offers us to be united to the Son and included in his death and resurrection?

Any time we look at our bodies with disdain at their very humanity, we reveal our impoverished theology of the incarnation. When we consider our frail form—the way our bodies get sick, grow lean with lack, and falter under the burden of physical suffering—and believe them to be less Christlike for their infirmities, we reveal our lackluster understanding of Christ's own suffering in his humanity. Christ became man, not to save us *from* every suffering in our bodies, but to save us eternally *through* suffering in his. One day he will deliver us from these bodies bound to die in resurrection power. One day, our physical suffering will be put to an end all because Jesus suffered on our behalf.

But that's not the only promise he offers us. The hope Christ gives us is not only far-off in eternity, but can be embraced and experienced in our sufferings today. Because of his life, death, and resurrection, our suffering now is shot through with new meaning and this hope-filled promise: though we suffer, we never suffer alone.

When our bodies limp and ache, when they fall ill and quiver with weakness, we have the joy of looking to Jesus, remembering that there is no suffering we experience that he cannot meet us in. His suffering is ever deeper. When our bodies, failing and frail, sink into the darkness of physical death, we do not hear the voice of our Savior asking us to spiritually supersede our suffering. We will not hear his voice asking for us to believe more or pray harder. We will hear the whisper of his Spirit and the witness of the Scriptures:

> *He himself bore our sins in his body on the tree, that*
> *we might die to sin and live to righteousness. By his*
> *wounds you have been healed. (1 Pet. 2:24)*

Hands and Feet Ministry

Our calling as members of Christ's body is to be fit together in such a way that we more closely resemble our risen Savior. Our journey of personal and corporate sanctification is to look more like Jesus. One day, he has promised to return and to glorify his church, and his own resurrection stands as a promise and guarantee that we will follow in his life-giving footsteps. When he does, we will not limp and stumble, as the body corporate and our own physical forms do today. But we will see him face-to-face, and we will look like him (1 John 3:2).

Until then, we stretch. We press. We tenderly push one another to look more like Jesus.

God has left us with a commission, a charge that should occupy every day there is breath in our lungs: as the body of Christ, we are to live as his hands and feet. Wherever there is hurt, we tend the wounds. Wherever there is weakness, we treasure, guard, and keep. Wherever there is sickness, we nourish and nurse back to health, Lord willing.

The work of ministry on this side of the resurrection is to be the physical presence of God in this world. Our theology of the incarnation touches down in our lives of discipleship and worship as we live into Christ's commissioning that sends us into the earth to bear his presence as his body to the lost world yet apart from him.

And we will not be surprised to find that it is an embodied ministry.

The ministry that holds the hand of a young mother defeated by her own habitual sin and reminds her that Christ overcame sin and death. The ministry that sits in the doctor's office with the father of three children as he receives news of a life-ending diagnosis, and in the tears and the sorrow, softly proclaims in hope that death has never been the end for the body of Jesus. The ministry that waits in the dark hour of fear and doubt with the young believer who wonders if God is real, if he really came to save, if he really is present in the world and insists, yes, he is. By his Spirit, he is right here.

When the darkness of sin and the Fall enshrouded all of creation, when every human heart was filled with fear and dread, when we were no better off than a child waking in the middle of the night with terrors all around, God sent his Son. Our incarnated Savior made God fully known to our fallen humanity, and has given us the ministry of doing the same. Together, we bear witness to the God who came, died, rose again and returned to his Father that we might know God personally and proclaim him in unison. The physical body of Christ, given for the body of Christ, that we might proclaim and carry the very presence of God.

> The people who walked in darkness
>   have seen a great light;
> [Because] to us a child is born,
>   to us a son is given;
> and the government shall be upon his shoulder,
>   and his name shall be called
> Wonderful Counselor, Mighty God,
>   Everlasting Father, Prince of Peace.
> (Isa. 9:2, 6)

Pneumatology: Worshiping God the Spirit

Those in whom the Spirit comes to live are
God's new Temple. They are, individually and
corporately, places where heaven and earth meet.[1]
N. T. Wright

I t was a typical Sunday school hour in the little Baptist church
we attended. The children's lesson for the day was on the Holy
Ghost—who he is, what he does, and how he lives inside those
who believe. The class of second and third graders motioned
wildly as they recited their memory verse: "Do you not KNOW,"
they exclaimed, pointing to their heads, "that your BODY is the
TEMPLE of the HOLY SPIRIT"—each key word punctuated
by a memorable motion that sent most of them into an escalating
contest to see who could sign the grandest. Classic.

Before things got out of hand, the teacher had each child sit
on their carpet squares with their heads bowed and eyes closed,
and concluded her lesson with an invitation to invite Jesus and

---

[1] N. T. Wright, *Simply Christian: Why Christianity Makes Sense* (New York: HarperCollins, 2010), 129.

his Spirit "into your heart." Little girls in knit tights and Mary Janes and little boys with disheveled clip-on ties peered through squinting eyes as the teacher led the class in praying a version of the sinner's prayer, each child waving their hands wildly when she asked who had prayed along with her.

All hands seemed to wriggle in the air excitedly—all except one. One little second grader, Micah, sat in the back picking at his carpet square and squirming under the watchful gaze of his teacher. His hand was decidedly not raised.

"Micah," she asked, pulling him aside as the class was dismissed. "What do you think about Jesus being your Savior?"

"Good," came his one-word, unenthusiastic response as he avoided eye contact.

"Well then, why didn't you want to pray with the rest of the class to invite Jesus into your heart?"

"*Because*," he sighed exasperated, his whole body dropping with the relief of confession. "I don't want no *ghost* living inside of me!"

Micah is more honest than the rest of us.

Honest Confusion

If you've been in the church for any length of time, you may have noticed that different church traditions deal with this Holy Ghost very differently. Some traditions make the Spirit the center of their worship gatherings and theology. They might even be offended or baffled to speak of a "theology" of the Spirit because the concept seems to dry out the richness of their spiritual experience with him. To these ears, defining a doctrine of the Holy Spirit is akin to a third grader putting together her insect report for school: in order to pin down the project, you have to kill the object of your study.

On the other end of the spectrum, some traditions seem to avoid discussing the Spirit altogether; these churches love the defined lines of doctrine, and the mysterious nature of the Spirit doesn't exactly seem to fix in any given theological box. And so while the Spirit is welcomed in statements of faith and doctrine, they're not entirely sure he has a place in Sunday's worship service (and they might turn a skeptical eye toward those who ask about his inclusion).

Wherever your own practice falls along the spectrum, there is one thing most of us have in common: a theology of the Holy Spirit confuses and confounds us. We, like Micah, aren't entirely sure what it would mean for the Spirit of God to dwell within us, and so we leave our hands in our laps and avoid eye contact when asked to articulate our theology of the Spirit (formally known as pneumatology).

But we are those who are convinced that theology is a study of God—It's the practice of looking to God's Word and articulating true things about God's nature and Person. And, as such, the Spirit of God cannot be left out; it is altogether appropriate to talk about a theology of the Spirit because the Spirit himself is the *theos* of our ology—the God of our study.

We cannot have a healthy theology of the Father and of Christ and lose steam by the time we arrive at the discussion of the Spirit. We don't want to be those who wave our hand in dismissal at this doctrine because we're either confused or intimidated; we don't want to lack clarity on the topic of the Spirit because the mystery of his nature, work, and person seems too thick for us to hold in biblical tension.

He is, after all, the third person of the Trinity. And we are Trinitarian people.

A Heritage of Confusion

Before we get into clarifying what we believe about the Spirit of God, it's worth confessing why confusion on this topic exists. It's not laziness that has rendered us theologically lacking on the topic. It isn't simply the divergent denominations that aid our confusion about the Spirit of God. The pages of God's Word leave us grappling with the mystery of who God is in his Spirit. More than any other person of the Trinity, the Spirit is referred to in metaphor and simile throughout the Bible.

The Spirit inverts Old Testament expectations by not coming in wind or earthquake or fire, but in a still, small voice (1 Kings 19). The Spirit appeared at Jesus' baptism in the form of a dove (Matt. 3). The Spirit sprang up in tongues "like flames of fire" hovering over believers' heads at Pentecost (Acts 2 csb). As Gordon Fee would say, "Listen to our images: dove, wind, fire, water, oil. No wonder many regard the Spirit as a gray, oblong blur and find him so difficult to understand and to relate to."[2]

These Holy Spirit passages tend to leave us confused—and confusion has always been uncomfortable for us. Because we can't quite wrap our minds around these eternal truths, we have opted to avoid them instead, and the result is theologically devastating: in light of the metaphors about the Spirit, we move away from a relational understanding of the Spirit in favor of a distant, muddied view of the Spirit of God or a hyper-dramatized view of his nature. We forget him as the third person of the Trinity, and we rush about our spiritual lives with a much greater theological focus on the Father and the Son to the diminishment of the Holy Ghost, letting him linger in the unformed margins of our theological lives. We treat him like the dusty pile of family photos in the attic that we'll get to organizing someday—it's important, special, and sacred, we know; but it's not something we want to deal with right now, and every time he comes to mind, he feels a bit overwhelming.

And yet we know better. We know that to subtract the Spirit of God from the Trinitarian God we worship renders him not at all himself. It leaves us with an eternal Father who does not lift our eyes to him; with a Savior who does not dwell within his people. Michael Bird puts it well: "Theological study without the

---

[2] Gordon D. Fee, *Paul, the Spirit, and the People of God* (Grand Rapids: Baker Academic, 2011), 25.

Holy Spirit behind it would be drier than a James Bond martini. The Holy Spirit reminds us that we are not studying divine ideas but encountering divine persons, that faith is cognitive as well as charismatic, and that exegesis and experience go together."[3]

Third Person of the Trinity

Our theological foundation of a Trinitarian God reminds us that the third person of the Godhead is the Holy Spirit. As such, everything we know about God's character—his eternality, love, and relational nature—is rightly applied to our understanding of the Spirit. What we can know about God's triune nature guides and guards our theology of the Spirit.

In many ways, this is the best place to start: to say what we can about the triune God and let our minds use those attributes as building blocks in our doctrine of the Spirit. The Spirit is limitless, all-powerful, all-knowing, and all-present. No one and nothing created him; he relies on nothing and no one for sustenance. He is, as a person of the Godhead, self-sustaining, self-ruling, and self-loving in the happy land of the Trinity. Rightly camped in the context of his triune nature, the Spirit of God loses some of the fogginess that aids us in keeping him at arm's length.

And still the Spirit is distinct in his work from the Father and the Son. Just as the Father and Son are distinct Persons who have particular roles to play in the story of redemption, so it is with the Spirit of God. So what does his work look like?

Many of us think of the work of the Spirit predominately in terms of New Testament activity. It's easy to think that the Spirit of God was mostly inactive throughout the Old Testament (though we'll admit he showed up time and again to speak

---

[3] Michael F. Bird, *What Christians Ought to Believe: An Introduction to Christian Doctrine Through the Apostles' Creed* (Grand Rapids: Zondervan, 2016), 191.

through a prophet), and then we watch him burst onto the scene in the book of Acts with vigor. Our contemporary readings of the entire Bible can lead us to assume that the Spirit was sitting on the Old Testament sidelines until God decided to put him in the game in the final quarter to really wow the crowds.

But since we believe in a triune God, we know this can't be the case. Instead, anywhere we see the presence of God throughout the Old and New Testaments we can rest assured: the Spirit of God is there. From the first page to the last, the Spirit of God is on every page of Scripture, doing an ongoing work that he began at the dawn of creation and bringing the redemptive plan of God into final fullness. Like a stream that you can trace to a river and watch it spill out into the ocean, so we can trace the work and person of the Spirit of God from Genesis to Revelation.

Personal Presence

As we wade into the theological waters concerning the Holy Spirit, it's helpful to consider the ways in which the Spirit of God has been at work in the Old Testament so that we can trace it into the New. And, we might be surprised to find that the Spirit of God doesn't just show up in the first book of the Bible, but on the very first lines of Scripture. As the dawn of the first creation day was spoken into existence, we're told that God created the heavens and the earth. While this is a general statement about God's activity, the Bible gets rather specific right away. Telling us about particular activities occurring at the time of creation, Genesis 1:2 reads:

> *Now the earth was formless and empty, darkness was over the surface of the deep, and the Spirit of God was hovering over the waters. (NIV)*

Does it surprise you to find that the first mention of a specific person of the Trinity is the Spirit? While God triune is doing the creative work, the Spirit in particular is moving throughout creation. It is in God's nature to move toward his creation; as we've seen, this is an outflowing of the loving nature inherent within his Trinitarian being. And it's the Spirit of God specifically who is present in the creation story, hovering in proximity to the created world. He doesn't keep his divine distance. He doesn't oversee or supervise. He is mysteriously active and ardently present in the created world.

This is the work we will see on every page of the Scriptures. We can trace this habit of God's from Genesis to Revelation: God moves toward his people, and he does so by his Spirit as he leads them, calls them, and secures them.

People of the Presence-Lost

As we make our way through the Old Testament narratives, we find that even east of Eden, God's presence pursues his people. Though mankind falls into sin and away from the presence of God, God, in his saving, rescuing nature, calls his people back to himself. And he does this through the call of Abraham.

We'll notice that God doesn't call Abraham to found a particular religion, per se, but calls him to "walk before [him]" (Gen. 17:1 NIV). This is God's way of calling Abraham to live his entire life in God's holy presence, to relate to him in worship, and revere him as his God. Abraham's calling is all about proximity to the presence of God. Abraham was called out from among his kindred people to be a man marked by relationship to Yahweh. Abraham would live his life differently, look different than his neighbors and nephew, and go places he never expected all because he was met by the presence of God and it marked his life.

And it didn't stop there. Abraham's offspring—brought about by the powerful provision of God—grows into a great nation, the nation of Israel. Though their journey takes them into Egyptian captivity, where for a long season of suffering they lose their identity as God's chosen people, God calls them out and makes them his own people once again. He does this through remarkable and miraculous means (some may even call them "signs and wonders") that reveal the power of God's Spirit and the claim he has on his people. He turns water to blood, causes a locust infestation, and moves in the heart of Pharaoh in such a way that God is ultimately glorified and the people of God go free.

As God draws his people out into freedom, their identity as a people is reformed. Those who had been owned as slaves and trampled down as the possession of Pharaoh were now called to be a united people. And what is to be their national conception as a people? What marks them? What bands them together in national identity and alliance? The presence of God. The people of God will come to know themselves unequivocally as "the people of the presence" (Exod. 33:12–17).

Take No Substitutes

Being a "people of the presence" became so core to Israel's national and corporate identity that Moses knows no substitute for the Spirit of God will suffice. After God has called his people into covenant relationship with himself—a call that included his promise to dwell among them in the tabernacle—a devastating event occurs in the life of God's people. While Moses is away actively receiving construction instructions from God, the people of the presence fail to live into their new identity. They reject the invisible mark of the invisible God. They want more than the Spirit; they want something tangible. And so they build themselves an idol.

> [Aaron] took what [the Israelites] handed him and made it into an idol cast in the shape of a calf, fashioning it with a tool. Then they said, "These are your gods, Israel, who brought you up out of Egypt." (Exod. 32:4 NIV)

"These are your gods, Israel . . ." The words must have hung thickly in the air as the stomachs of all faithful Israelites plummeted in despair. The people wanted a god they could see, touch, and bow to. They demanded a god formed and fashioned—one who didn't loom with so much mystery and so beyond their sight and comprehension. A god they could carry with them, tuck safely under their arms on the journey without having to wonder when he would show up next and where he might unexpectedly lead them.

And so the true God gives them exactly what they demand. God tells Moses that the results of their rebellion will lead to the granting of their request: God's Spirit will no longer go before them. "My Presence will not go with you," God says, in essence; an angel will be sent ahead of them instead (Exod. 33:1–3).

At first blush, this punishment may not seem so devastating. After all, an angel could provide guidance, right? An angel could lead them to the land, no? But even though we may not realize the magnitude of this statement, Moses does. Moses knows that this secondary option is no substitute for the presence of God himself.[4] This is why he cries out before God:

> *The LORD replied, "My Presence will go with you,*
> *and I will give you rest." Then Moses said to him,*
> *"If your Presence does not go with us, do not send us*
> *up from here. How will anyone know that you are*
> *pleased with me and with your people unless you go*
> *with us? What else will distinguish me and your*
> *people from all the other people on the face of the*
> *earth?" (Exod. 33:14–16 NIV, emphasis mine)*

---

[4] Throughout the Old Testament, Yahweh is present in the Angel of the LORD. Passages like Exodus 23:20–22; Judges 13:16–22; cf. Genesis 48:15–16 remind us that God's presence isn't entirely distinguished from the Angel in several instances. The point for our purposes is, however, that Moses is not satisfied until he knows that God *himself* is going with them.

A messenger for God is no substitute for God's very own presence leading his people by his Spirit. Why is this solution so inadequate? Because the people of the Presence would cease to be who they are without the Spirit of God.[5]

Saving Presence of God

This is the first time we see God's people foolishly hope to trade the Spirit of God for a shoddy alternative; but it will not be the last. In fact, this is the pattern we see repeated throughout the Old Testament narratives: God's people repeatedly distanced themselves from God by their sin and rebellion, and God consistently moves toward his people to rescue them from their sin and restore them to his presence.

And it wasn't a vague concept of his presence that saved them. It wasn't a mere notion of his nearness that brought them out of trouble. It was the very Spirit of God.

This is why the prophet Isaiah reflects on Israel's fitful walk with God this way:

> . . . and he [God] became their savior
>   in all their distress.
> **It was no messenger or angel**
>   **but his presence that saved them;**
> in his love and in his pity he redeemed them;
>   he lifted them up and carried them all the days
>   of old.
> But they rebelled
>   **and grieved his holy spirit;**
> therefore he became their enemy;
>   he himself fought against them.
> Then they remembered the days of old,
>   of Moses his servant.

---

[5] Fee, *Paul, the Spirit, and the People of God*, 13.

Where is the one who brought them up out of the sea
  with the shepherds of his flock?
Where is the one who put within them his holy
  spirit,
who caused his glorious arm
  to march at the right hand of Moses,
who divided the waters before them
  to make for himself an everlasting name,
  who led them through the depths?
Like a horse in the desert,
  they did not stumble.
Like cattle that go down into the valley,
  the spirit of the LORD gave them rest.
Thus you led your people,
  to make for yourself a glorious name.
(Isa. 63:8b–14 NRSV, emphasis mine)

Did you catch that? God assures Moses that his very own presence will go before them and that *he* will give them rest, and the culmination of this promise is revealed in Isaiah's proclamation: the Spirit of the Lord gave them rest. God's promise was kept; not in an intangible way, but by his Spirit.

God's presence among his people isn't vague or abstract; it's a person. The Holy Spirit, the third person of the Trinity, is God's grace among his people, the marker that sets them apart, and the primary means by which he leads, directs, and blesses them—both corporately and individually. And, when they fall into sin, it is by the withdrawing of the Spirit of God that God's presence is barred. This is why King David confesses his personal sin with Bathsheba before God and begs him, "do not cast me away from your presence, and do not take your Holy Spirit from me" (Ps. 51:11 NIV). And when David needs direction, he begs of God, "Teach me to do your will, for you are my God! Let your good Spirit lead me on level ground!" (Ps. 143:10).

The Work of Christ

Through the promised Savior, Jesus, God made a way for his people to reenter his presence once again. Because Jesus lived a sinless life, died a sacrificial death in our place, and rose to life again—because of who he is in his person and what he accomplished in his life and ministry—the way is now open for you and me and all who believe to be made right with God again. Through Christ, we can now enter God's presence covered in the Son's righteousness.

This is why Gospel authors go out of their way to emphasize the events that occurred on the darkest day of history, Good Friday. Though all the drama of the Passion narrative is happening at the Place of the Skull (where Jesus hung on a cross), Matthew and Luke make note of something that happened miles away as they pen the words that punctuate Christ's death:

> *And Jesus cried out again with a loud voice and yielded up his spirit. And behold, the curtain of the temple was torn in two, from top to bottom. (Matt. 27:50–51a)*

It is no coincidence that as Jesus breathed his final breath and committed his spirit to the Father in death that the curtain that separated the Holy of Holies—the place of God's dwelling among men—from the outer courts of the temple was torn in two. God was doing a new thing in Christ, a much-anticipated thing, a thing that broke open the previously established confines to God's holy presence. As Jesus stood in our place as the perfect, unblemished sacrifice for our sin, the way was opened for God's people to approach God's presence once again. Though our sin had chronically separated us from God's holy presence, God looked on the bloodied body of Christ as the final sacrifice required to atone for our sin. Because of Jesus, God's presence is made available to God's people once again.

Promise of Presence Restored

Reflecting on the work of Christ is overwhelming. Truly, nothing causes me to worship God more than reflecting on the person of Christ, his death, and resurrection. The disciples felt the same way, which is why, as they surrounded the risen Christ, they looked at him with bewilderment when he said he was going away again, and that *it was for their good*. He puts it this way:

> *"It is to your advantage that I go away; for if I do not go away, the Helper will not come to you. But if I go, I will send him to you." (John 16:7)*

Though humanity had been separated from God by their sin, because Christ's work was now complete there was hope restored that the presence of God would dwell among his people again. The promise of the risen Christ to his disciples illuminates the work he came to do: God himself was coming to them again. The Spirit of God would come to his people and mark them as his precious own once more.

"It is to your advantage . . ." Jesus insists. What could possibly be better than Jesus himself? What could ever be better than the incarnated Christ, Immanuel, God with us?

The Spirit. The Spirit was the *advantage* of which Jesus spoke so strongly. Jesus came to be God *with* us, but because of Christ's complete work, the Spirit would now be the Helper of God's people—God *in* us.

The Spirit's Ministry Today

Just as the Spirit loomed throughout creation at the dawn of time, the Spirit is at work in the world today. In Genesis, the Spirit of God moved toward God's creation, intentionally seeking proximity to God's people and world. He wanted to be *present*. Near. Close. *With*. And the same is true now. This is what the Spirit is up to in the world at this very moment. The Spirit of

God is at work in creation, calling the world to repentance (John 16:8), sending out witnesses to the work of Christ into all the earth (Acts 1:8), and revealing God's good and faithful character to those separated from God by sin (1 Cor. 2:10).

And the Spirit continues to build out a people of the presence. It was not just the nation of Israel that was marked by the presence of God in their midst; by the Spirit, God is building and uniting his church as his holy people (1 Cor. 12:13). The Spirit is calling God's people out from among the nations, setting us apart as holy, uniting us to one another, and creating for himself a people marked by the presence of God once again.

This is why the words of the Apostles' Creed resound with such joy as God's people confess, "I believe in the Holy Spirit, the Holy Catholic[6] Church, the communion of saints . . ." It's all too appropriate that these lines find themselves as neighboring truths in the historic confession; it is the Spirit of God that builds that universal church—a people set apart to God, consisting of a countless number of sinful individuals who will or already have turned to the Lord; a holy nation comprised of those from every nationality, tribe, tongue, and culture. It is the Spirit that causes all of these diverse, sinful, redeemed people to commune together under the one shared hope of salvation in Christ alone.

An Old New Work

Just as the Spirit was at work in the Old Testament, we find him up to the same wonderful activities in the New. And yet . . . we don't want to miss the *new* thing the Spirit is doing on

---

[6] At the time of this creed's writing, *catholic* here simply meant "universal." So, the "Holy Catholic Church" should be interpreted as the universal Church—God's people, in all times and all places, who have placed their faith exclusively in Jesus Christ as their Savior. This should be understood distinct from the Roman Catholic Church. The creed's intent is to reference believers in all times and all places, not to speak of a specific church tradition.

the pages of the New Testament as well. God "moved into the neighborhood,"[7] among his people in the time of the temple, and by the Spirit, God is now moving into the hearts of every believer who calls upon Christ. When we understand the magnitude of what God did at the temple dwelling (and all that was lost in Israel's rebellion and consequential loss of the temple), we read the words of Paul with new excitement:

> Or do you not know that your body is a temple of the
> Holy Spirit within you, whom you have from God?
> You are not your own . . . (1 Cor. 6:19)

God isn't just in the neighborhood anymore. He has taken up residence within each and every believer who places their faith in Christ. When we think back on the detailed instructions for the temple in the Old Testament—the fine needlework, the pure gold, the jewels inlaid in the very design on God's dwelling place—it should seem outlandish to you and I that the very presence of the holy God now dwells in us by his Spirit. God, in his extensive mercy and grace, has seen fit—no, has counted it a *joy*—to dwell in the hearts of those who are his. God's presence has been restored to his people, and as he dwells within his people, he is closer than he has ever been this side of Eden.

Promise of Permanent Presence

Every landlord I've had has always loved me (weird flex, I know). When I rented my first apartment in Chicago post-undergrad, the landlord skeptically asked me what time she could expect the unit to "quiet down" at night, a nod at her low expectations for twenty-one-year-old partiers. I gave her what must have been the blankest stare and told her without a hint of sarcasm: "I generally go to bed around 9:30 p.m."

---

[7] Eugene Peterson is commonly attributed with coining this phrase in his paraphrasing of John 1:14 (MSG).

Ever since, landlords have loved me. I'm a homebody, which means I'm clean and pretty quiet. I love following the rules, paying rent on time, and keeping neighbors happy, and those three things always seemed to seal the deal when applying for a new rental property.

But regardless of how great of a tenant I seemed at the outset, landlords are wise to cover their bases. This means that they wanted more from me than my word that I'd take good care of the place; they wanted a guarantee. They wanted more than a promise; they wanted a deposit.

So, for each apartment I rented, I put down a hefty chunk of change—a deposit that assured the landlord that I would keep up my end of the bargain. I'd take care of the unit I occupied, and if I failed to do so, I would forfeit my hard-earned cash.

As we trace the theme of God's presence from the Old Testament to the New, it's easy to stop on the pages of the book of Acts and revel in the glory of the indwelling Spirit—the Spirit who made God's people the people of the presence in the Old Testament, and who continues to make (and remake) us the people of his presence today. And yet, another promise awaits us. Those of us who live our lives in the Spirit now are a people who live in light of a promise that is yet to be fulfilled: one day, we will all live in the unhindered presence of God in the fullness of his glorious kingdom. One day, God will return to earth, make all things new, and bring all of his redemptive work to completion.

To be a Christian is to live with this hope: this is not all that there is. This world is not final. Even this delightful life in the Spirit is not the final set of affairs for the people of God. There awaits a final fulfillment, a fullness yet to be enjoyed. And our hope that God will keep this promise is firm. Why? Because God himself gave us a "deposit"—he gave us a sign that seals the deal that he will make good on his claim and come to us again.

> *Now He who establishes us with you in Christ and anointed us is God, who also sealed us and gave us* **the Spirit in our hearts as a pledge.** *(2 Cor. 1:21–22 NASB, emphasis mine)*

> *Now He who prepared us for this very purpose is God, who gave us* **the Spirit as a pledge.** *(2 Cor. 5:5 NASB, emphasis mine)*

God has done more than make a promise to dwell with his people in full. He has given us an assurance by giving us his Spirit. The guarantee that God will keep his end of the deal and redeem his people in full is the gift of his Spirit. And unlike the deposit that I always put down for each apartment, God stands to lose more than just a few dollars. The deposit of the Spirit means that for God to abandon his people and his redemptive plan, he would go back on his very pledge to his people. And to do that, God would have to cease being his promise keeping self, separating what he in his perfect and holy will has joined together. This is theologically unachievable! It's a divine impossibility! The pledge that God has given us in and by his Spirit fosters within us a sure, solid, concrete hope: we will dwell with God one day. We are bound to be people of the full presence of God—the very Spirit of God is our pledge.

Bond of Salvation

For all of us who have placed our faith in the person of Jesus Christ for salvation, the Spirit has already done an incredible work. The Scriptures teach us that it is by the Spirit that we recognize our need for a Savior, and confess that we are sinful and separated from God, and bears witness that Jesus is the only Savior who is able to set us free (John 15:26). Before you and I were likely ever aware of the doctrine of the Spirit, he was mysteriously, joyfully, and graciously at work in our lives, pointing us to the hope of our salvation: Jesus.

And the Spirit didn't stop there. But, at salvation, it is the Spirit who bonds us in faith to the person of Jesus Christ. Our union with the Son of God in salvation is accomplished in no other way than for the Spirit of Christ to come and dwell within us. This is why John Calvin wrote in *The Institutes* of the multifaceted reality of union with Christ, and how it comes about mysteriously by the Spirit of God.

> First, we must understand that as long as Christ remains outside of us, and we are separate from him, all that he has suffered and done for the salvation of the human race remains useless and of no value for us. Therefore to share with us what he has received from the Father he had to become ours and to dwell within us. For this reason, he is called "our head" (Eph. 4:15), and "the first-born among many brethren" (Rom. 8:29). We also, in turn, are said to be "engrafted into him" (Rom. 11:17) and to "put on Christ" (Gal. 3:27); for as I have said, all that he possesses is nothing to us until we grow into one body with him. It is true that we obtain this by faith. Yet since we see that not all indiscriminately embrace that communion with Christ which is offered through the gospel, reason itself teaches us to climb higher and to examine into the secret energy *of the Spirit, by which we come to enjoy Christ and all his benefits*.[8]

Calvin knew something we are prone to forget: the work of Christ is made accessible to us by the Spirit of God. What

---

[8] John Calvin, et al., *Institutes of the Christian Religion* (Louisville, KY: Westminster John Knox Press, 2011), emphasis added.

the good news about Jesus promises to us—life in Christ, ability to approach the throne of God in grace rather than judgment, etc.—is put into effect by the Spirit as he indwells us and makes us one with our Savior. It is explicitly by the Spirit of God that we cry out "Abba, Father"—we are able to approach the Father as such because the Spirit has made us one with the Son of God (Rom. 8:15).

Bird helps shed light on the way the Spirit applies the realities of the gospel to the life of every believer: "In salvation the Holy Spirit is both the giver and the gift itself. What the gospel promises, the Holy Spirit actualizes: life, love, joy, and peace. In our spiritual life, the Spirit speaks, leads, helps, witnesses, and even inhibits where necessary."[9] All the joys of the gospel, all the promises of God, all the righteousness of Christ is being applied to you and me today by the power of the indwelling Spirit of God. This is his ongoing ministry, the tasks he gladly takes up today as he sets us free from the law and gives us life in Christ (Rom. 8:2).

Not a First Name

I have never been a shy individual. Even when I was very young (or, perhaps, especially when I was very young), I had unearned confidence that could carry me for miles, and I often had to be put in my place. VBS 1996 was one such occasion. After confidently telling my peers that Christ was just the last name for Jesus, my teacher called me out. And I Did. Not. Like. it.

She gently corrected me, and I came back with all the authority of a seven-year-old know-it-all. I insisted that the pastor had told me *specifically*: Jesus is his first name, Christ is his last name. She drew a deep breath, crossed her arms over her chest, and called my mother.

---

[9] Bird, *What Christians Ought to Believe*, 191.

A quarter of a century later, I can confess: the pastor had not told me that. I had just heard the name "Jesus Christ" so often growing up that I didn't stop to question what the words in that title actually meant. Because the title was over-used, I under-appreciated the significance of his name, and missed the point altogether.

We are prone to doing the same thing with the Holy Spirit. While we know that "holy" isn't the Spirit's first name, we tend to forget the gravity of what this title means for us—both theologically and in our daily lives of discipleship. The Spirit of God is holy. He is without sin, blemish, mistake, or fault. He has no deceit in him, no propensity for unfaithfulness, no ability to rebel against his own perfect ways, which are, of course, the perfect ways of God. The Spirit of God is the *Holy* Spirit.

While we might embrace this reality theologically, we may neglect the weight of this theological reality for our lives. The Spirit that has taken up residence within the lives of Christians is a purified, perfect presence. It is why the ongoing work of the Spirit is to make us holy as God is holy (1 Pet. 1:16). As the Spirit of God resides within us, he forms us more and more into the image of the perfect Son of God, who is also perfectly holy. We call this work sanctification; the Spirit who God has sent to dwell within us helps us in our weakness (Rom. 8:26), enables us to keep God's commands (John 14:15), and continually sets us free from sin (2 Cor. 3:17).

The Spirit of God dwelling in us makes us more like God day by day. And what's more? He doesn't only help us do the right things, but he is at work to make us into the right *people*. He doesn't live in us to operate us like a robot, helping us behave more appropriately and make the best choices by working our internal controls; his work is a *regenerating* work (Titus 3:5). The Holy Spirit reforms and restores and reshapes the marred image of God in us that was fractured by the Fall, back into the image of Christ, giving us hearts of flesh instead of stone (Ezek. 36:26–27), helping us to love God (John 14:15), guiding us in truth (John 16:13), and pouring the love of God into our hearts (Rom. 5:5). As he dwells within us, he is making us holy just as he is holy.

Fruits and Gifts

Because the Spirit's work is vast and glorious, it should come as no surprise, then, that the New Testament uses such promising language when describing the evidence of the Spirit's work. While much of what the Spirit does is unseen, the outworking of his ministry is described as *fruit* and *gifts*. And we can't help but notice that both of these words are hope-filled words. They're words to be savored, and received with joy and gratitude.

One of my favorite places on earth is Wilson's Apple Orchard in small-town, Iowa. We would go to this orchard on nearly a weekly basis in the fall when we were children, and we got to know Mr. Wilson and his white-haired wife like family. Our troop of nine kids and two parents would drive out of town and park just outside the orchard property. There, Mr. Wilson's wrinkled, leathery hands would hand us our baskets and send us out into the property to pick apples to our heart's content with only one caveat: we could only pick what was in season.

I know it's hard to imagine, but patience was hard for me as a child. And if I was told that I had to wait for something, I wanted it all the more. So when Mr. Wilson would tell me that today was a day for picking Marigolds, all I wanted was a Macintosh.

Thankfully, Mr. Wilson knew a secret after his eighty years of orchard farming and managing troublemakers like myself: it only takes one bite of an under-ripe apple to teach a lesson. For me, it may have taken a few bites before I got it through my stubborn head, but eventually I learned the lesson. Good fruit takes time. It doesn't come on demand, and it requires more patience than my ten-year-old self-possessed.

As the Spirit makes us holy ("sanctifies" us), the Scriptures tell us that he bears fruit in our lives. The outworking of the

Spirit's residence in our hearts shows up in the spiritual fruit our lives bear. And the fruit of the Spirit? Well, it's all good fruit.

> *But the fruit of the Spirit is love, joy, peace, patience, kindness, goodness, faithfulness, gentleness, self-control. (Gal. 5:22–23a)*

The spiritual produce God brings about in our lives is *good*—each and every attribute that he cultivates in our lives is proclaimed of the character of God throughout the Scriptures. The Spirit makes us like himself, causing us to be loving as he is loving, granting us spirits of joy as he is a Spirit of joy, and giving us peace just like he is peace.

But he doesn't do this work instantaneously at the time of our conversion. Just like Mr. Wilson, the Spirit of God takes his time and allows the fruit to be cultivated within us. While our salvation by grace through faith in Jesus is immediate, our sanctification takes time. How tender of God to approach our holiness this way. How patient and long-suffering he is to call us to salvation and then do the long-term work of making us more like him progressively, painstakingly, and attentively. As he dwells within my heart and yours, the Spirit of God is patiently at work, taking the seeds of our faith, growing them into an abundant harvest over time, and making us more like himself.

As we grow in our relationship with Christ and in the life of discipleship, we should see these attributes budding in our lives. While we will not be made perfect this side of the new heaven and new earth, we are bound to see a sprig of gentleness spring up where once there was only bitterness and entitlement. We can watch for a sapling of faithfulness growing where we used to be self-interested and unenduring. The Spirit will cultivate within our hearts evidence of his presence, and there will be fruit in our lives that shows the world: the Spirit of God is really here. He's really made this body his home.

Fruitful Gifts

Even as the Spirit bears fruit in our lives individually, he is also about the business of cultivating the church communally. This is why he gives his people gifts—spiritual blessings that aid the body of Christ in walking faithfully, living for eternity, and binding God's people together in unity. The primary place we read about the gifts of the Spirit are in Paul's New Testament letters as he explains to new believers how they are to live lives of mutual service together for the glory of God. Paul tells the believers that each of them has been given spiritual gifts that are for the benefit of one another. He writes:

> Now there are varieties of gifts, but the same Spirit;
> and there are varieties of service, but the same Lord;
> and there are varieties of activities, but it is the
> same God who empowers them all in everyone. To
> each is given the manifestation of the Spirit for the
> common good. For to one is given through the Spirit
> the utterance of wisdom, and to another the utter-
> ance of knowledge according to the same Spirit, to
> another faith by the same Spirit, to another gifts of
> healing by the one Spirit, to another the working of
> miracles, to another prophecy, to another the abil-
> ity to distinguish between spirits, to another vari-
> ous kinds of tongues, to another the interpretation
> of tongues. All these are empowered by one and the
> same Spirit, who apportions to each one individu-
> ally as he wills. (1 Cor. 12:4–11)

Paul wants to make something extensively clear: the gifts of the Spirit look different, but the same Spirit is dwelling within each of them. And how are they to use these gifts? "For the common good." Believers are to use what has been entrusted to them—whether a spirit of discernment or gift of faith—so that the body of Christ is built up, fortified, and continually bettered by their service to one another.

Peter furthers this call by telling the believers that the gifts that the Spirit has given them are more than just a gift *for* them—they are gifts *entrusted to* them. He writes:

> *As each has received a gift, use it to serve one another, as good stewards of God's varied grace: whoever speaks, as one who speaks oracles of God; whoever serves, as one who serves by the strength that God supplies—in order that in everything God may be glorified through Jesus Christ. To him belong glory and dominion forever and ever. Amen. (1 Pet. 4:10–11)*

Christians don't have the luxury of using the gifts of the Spirit for self-interest or self-gain (in fact, Paul gets pretty specific about this in his letter to the church in Corinth). We are not the destination of the gifts, we are channels who receive them from God and then share them in service with our community. We are stewards of what has been entrusted to us, and we are to receive these gifts as they are—a grace of God for the benefit of the body of Christ to the glory of God.

Proper Caution

This emphasis is not a byline in the conversation on the gifts of the Spirit; it is at the heart of the Spirit's ministry. We can't forget that the Spirit is all about building the church and pointing to the glory of God—which means our ministry in the Spirit should always resemble his. This is why it is a travesty when abuses are done in the name of the Spirit. When people (particularly when those in a position of influence) misuse the name of God, attributing self-interested words to the call of God or work of the Spirit, it grieves the heart of God. When preachers tell the poor that God is calling them to "sow a seed of faith" through financial giving so that they or their loved one might be healed, or spiritual power is promised to those who buy into a particular brand of Christian dogma, it abandons the true ministry of the Spirit.

Throughout the book of Acts we see the most incredible works done by the Spirit of God. They are called "signs and wonders." And they're not called this arbitrarily. The work of the Spirit stands as a sign to those who are outside of the faith: a giant, flashing arrow to the power of God for salvation. The Spirit's miraculous work in creation is a marquee to those apart from Christ: *come find salvation in Christ! There is salvation in no other!*

Similarly, the Spirit causes believers to wonder at the work of God. The miracles the Spirit does in the book of Acts and his ongoing ministry around the world today make our jaws drop and remind us: there is no God like our God. The "signs and wonders" of the Spirit point definitively to God's saving power; they are a gift to the church and not to be abused in self-interest or self-promotion. They fix our eyes on God, the source, and keep us from being fixated on man, the channel.

Perhaps you're like me. You've seen the abuses of those who claim to do things in the name of the Spirit, but the result is bad fruit. The end of the event is always self-interested, and it makes you wonder if the Spirit is really at work in the world in these kinds of miraculous ways.

You and I can take great comfort in a simple litmus test: the Spirit will always bear witness to Christ (John 15). The work of the Spirit will always illuminate the saving work of Christ, will glory in his holiness and divinity, and will always leave people turning their faces toward the goodness of Jesus. Where the Spirit of God is at work, there will be signs pointing people to Jesus and wonders aiding people in the worship of God. Because the Spirit is the Spirit of Christ, his work will always testify to the power and majesty of the Savior.

A Life of Discipleship in the Spirit

God calls each believer to a life of faith and formation: a faith that clings to Christ in salvation, and a lifelong journey of formation as we are shaped and reshaped into Christ's likeness. And he hasn't left us this call without also leaving us his help. It is no accident that Jesus called the Spirit "the Helper" (John 15:26). It is the Spirit who helps us cling to Christ in faith, opening our eyes to our need for a Savior, and revealing to our broken hearts whose only fitting Savior is Jesus Christ. It is the Spirit who dwells within us at the moment of our confession and conversion, giving us new life in Jesus and beginning a lifelong work of remaking us in the likeness of our new Savior.

It is the Spirit who is the Comforter to us in our grief and sorrow; the One who draws close to us the presence of God in our lonely nights and dark stretches of grief (John 14:16–18). It is the Spirit who prays for us and with us and through us when the circumstances of life have robbed us of our ability to articulate our prayers to God (Rom. 8:26). And it is the Spirit—oh what a help to us!—who is our Counselor, training our feet in the ways of God and directing our steps in the paths of wisdom (Isa. 30:21).

These theological realities are not just for books and essays but meet us in the grit of our day-to-day lives. When you feel alone in this world and everything around you increases your sense of inner isolation, you can rest assured: you are not alone. If you have placed your faith in Jesus Christ, the Spirit of God has taken up residence within you. You cannot be abandoned. You will not be forsaken. You have a constant companion and partner in the Spirit of God who dwells within you.

In the moments when you feel that your propensity toward sin is overwhelming, when you feel as though there is no hope or way out of the temptation that haunts you day-by-day, you can take comfort: you are not left to your own strength. God has not called you to produce holiness in yourself of your own strength or effort. He has given you himself, his Holy Spirit, to dwell within you and make you holy.

When you fear that you will be fooled by charlatans who claim the name of the Spirit of power, but are seeking their own self-serving interest, you can have this confidence: God has given you his very Spirit of discernment and direction. He has not concealed his character and ways from you, but has given you his Word for your edification, his church for your safeguard, and his Spirit for your guidance.

If you have hustled hard and amassed for yourself an unbearable amount of responsibility and influence only to fear that you will let it all spin wildly out of control, you can take this to heart: you are not really in control. The same Spirit that hovered over the waters of creation is at work in this world beyond your imagination and wildest dreams. And while he is at work on the grand scale of the universe, executing his will and bringing glory to God, he is also intimately at work in the details of your life today.

Already, Not Yet

The Spirit is actively, intimately, personally at work in our lives today in all these ways and more. And yet this is just a foreshadowing of the hope that is to come. In the new heavens and new earth, God will finally and fully remake us as the people of his presence. We will live in the glorious reality of God's unhindered presence.

The book of Revelation pictures this final consummation of all things like a bride and groom finally coming together on their wedding day. The people of God are described as a bride who has been prepared, beautified, and purified for the day on which she will be united with her husband finally, fully, and forever. Christ is described as a groom who has come to bring her to himself.

We have the assurance that this wedding day will be a reality for the people of God. The deposit of this promise is the Spirit of God, God himself dwelling within us and readying us for that day. As we live our lives in the Spirit today, we live into the theological reality of what is "already and not yet"—we are already made one with Christ by the Spirit here and now in so many ways, and at the same time, that union is not yet fully realized. We live our lives of discipleship between these worlds— what God has already accomplished in Christ, and the hope of that work being perfected and complete at the wedding feast of the Lamb.

In this "in between" season of discipleship, we are members of the bride of Christ, who is being readied and beautified and purified by the sanctifying work of the Spirit. And, we have the privilege of looking toward that day with an exclamation of invitation to the world apart from God: Come!

> *The Spirit and the bride say, "Come." Let anyone who hears this say, "Come." Let anyone who is thirsty come. Let anyone who desires drink freely from the water of life. (Rev. 22:17 NLT)*

5

Soteriology: Worshiping the God Who Saves

And because of him you are in Christ Jesus,
who became to us wisdom from God,
righteousness and sanctification and redemption.
1 Corinthians 1:30

I could see the weariness tucked behind her glasses. Having stepped out to get the mail at an opportune moment, my day intersected with our letter carrier's. We had spoken in passing before, but today I took a stab at a bit of a deeper question, and her weariness unraveled like the bottom hems of her yoga pants in the winter slush. She had worked countless hours on the heels of Black Friday as more and more packages loaded down her truck. With a blank and tired stare, she shared that her company was not hiring extra workers for the upcoming holiday season, which meant that if she took a day off, she would fall behind on her routes. Without a sub, she would be left with an even fuller truck the day following her day of respite.

I could hear the tiredness in her voice, and my heart sank for her. Knowing seasons similar, I encouraged her to take a day off anyhow. To find some sort of a break. To step away from her work so that she wouldn't be consumed by it.

She thanked me politely, said she would consider it, and drove away in her truck. I returned to my day of work with a fresh armful of junk mail and bills, and fired up a quick prayer for my new friend to find a way to take some time off.

The small pile of mail was mostly rubbish, but it did contain a bill I had been waiting for. It was the final maternity bill due to the hospital, and, as I was ready to put these payments behind me, I wrote the check immediately, and addressed and stamped the envelope. The following morning I trotted out to the mailbox, shuffling my slippered feet, and taking care not to step on any outlying patches of winter ice. I dropped the bill in the mailbox, and raised the flag with a mental pat on my own back for being such a responsible adult as I skirted back inside.

As I went about my day, my gaze would happen upon the mailbox at the end of the drive. As I passed through the living room I would steal a peek at the box. The flag was still up. Later as I picked up lunch dishes, I peered out the windows. The flag was still up. But it was no worry; sometimes mail wasn't retrieved until after 4 p.m., so I had time left to wait. Three o'clock, 4 o'clock, and 5 o'clock all rolled by, and still the flag was unflinchingly raised.

Now, don't mistake me for a crazy lady. I'm not usually this attuned to the letter carrier's schedule, but for some reason this one gripped me. I was eager to see that white envelope whisked away along with my responsibility to our local maternity ward. Exasperated, I complained to my husband over dinner, "Why in the world has our mail not been picked up yet? It's nearly 7 o'clock!"

Austin's eyes darted at the ceiling for a split second as he recollected: "Didn't you encourage the letter carrier to take the day off?"

I gulped. Of course I had. Images of that weary woman flooded my memory, and my own quick prayer rang in my ears.

Hadn't she told me that this is exactly what would happen if she took a day off? Hadn't she lamented there were no subs? Wasn't I experiencing something I already knew—that for her to take time away would put packages and mail on hold while she took the time to rest?

In the end, I was glad she took the time off, and by the time she had retrieved the letter the next day I had nearly forgotten my anxiety over the outgoing bill. Outside yet again as she pulled to the mailbox, I cheered her on for her absence the day prior (and perhaps it was all in my mind, but I may have discerned a little pep in her step as she returned to her truck).

Looking back, I now see more clearly: I had mentally separated who my letter carrier *is* from what she *does*. Though she is known by her vocation—"letter carrier" is quite a forthcoming job title—carrying letters is not who she is. It is what she does; it is her *work*. When she, in her person, told me about her weariness, I encouraged her to rest, but I gave myself away as I waited for her at that mailbox the next day. At the bottom, I reduced my relationship to her to the service she provided me, not who she is as a person. And it was just this dissected approach that led me to do something quite foolish.

It seems to come more naturally to us as humans than we might like to admit—this business of dichotomizing a person's work from their person. Imagine with me a woman is single and craves all the benefits of having a husband. Living alone, she is reminded every time she changes a high-perched light bulb or carries groceries up three flights of steps to her apartment that the ample help her married friends enjoy is absent in her life. She files her taxes in April and wishes for the tax break a spouse would afford her. She budgets her income each month with a distant desire for someone else to add to the monthly bank account as well.

And so she does something that seems altogether reasonable: she marries. She meets and marries a man who will provide to her all the things she longs for. He will help around the house, he will supplement the income, he will walk the dog when it's raining and start her car when it's cold. He'll take three of six grocery bags up the apartment complex stairs and his very status in her life will save her a few dollars the next time April rolls around.

It's everything she wanted—except him. She doesn't want him or love him. There is nothing about who he is in his person that is desirable to her.

His work is what interested her. His person she could take or leave.

Here's the question in front of us in this chapter: Is that marriage? Is that a holy union?

A Dissected Gospel

The gospel is good news: God saves undeserving sinners by grace through faith in his Son, Jesus (Eph. 2:8–9). Our theology of salvation unpacks the bounty contained within this statement—how sinners are made sons, how the lost are found, how God looks on the sacrifice of his Son as sufficient payment for sins. At its core, this is one of the most foundational doctrines of the Christian life because it is likely the first we understood (even if in part) as we learned of our sin and our need for a Savior.

But sometimes the way we talk about the gospel is just as disjointed as my relationship to my letter carrier or our hypothetical woman's faux marriage. We speak of salvation as if it is merely a benefit we receive from Christ, a *work* he procures on our behalf. We look at the cross and the empty tomb and rejoice in what he has accomplished for us, but we do so in such a way that it is somehow dissected from his *person*. We approach salvation like the poor metaphor often offered in children's Sunday school classes: Christ has a gift (salvation) and he's holding it out to you; all you have to do it simply take it from him.

But Scripture doesn't actually speak of salvation in this way. Does it surprise you to find that salvation isn't a benefit that Christ affords to us, but something he offers *in his very self*?

Salvation isn't a gift that he worked hard to earn only to hand it off to you and me as we place our faith in him; he *is* the gift. Salvation isn't merely a task Jesus came to accomplish or a service he came to provide us—he himself is our salvation. Yes, benefits galore flow from his work of salvation, but the primary benefit is being united to the *worker* himself.

This doctrine is called union with Christ, and even if the term is unfamiliar to you, you're likely familiar with all the places it arises in Scripture. In speaking of our salvation, Paul emphatically speaks of believers being "in Christ." Over and over in the New Testament, in any place we find the theology of salvation taught, we find that being united to the person of Christ is the soul of the gospel:

> *Therefore, if anyone is* **in Christ**, *he is a new creation. The old has passed away; behold, the new has come. (2 Cor. 5:17, emphasis mine)*

> *For* **in Christ Jesus** *you are all sons of God, through faith. (Gal. 3:26, emphasis mine)*

> *And this is the testimony, that God gave us eternal life, and* **this life is in his Son**. *Whoever* **has the Son** *has life; whoever does not have the Son of God does not have life. (1 John 5:11–12, emphasis mine)*

> *When Christ* **who is your life** *appears, then you also will appear with him in glory. (Col. 3:4, emphasis mine)*

For most of my life, my theology of salvation was more akin to my relationship with my letter carrier—or the fictitious single gal's view of marriage—than it was to New Testament teachings on salvation. I thought of salvation like a trophy Christ won in his race against sin and death, which he, at the eternal finish line, passes off to us to place on our own spiritual shelves. Or, like a penniless vagabond, we come to Christ who has storehouses full of riches and wealth, which he generously shares with us. But this is not how the Bible conceives of our salvation. In fact, this is a grossly impoverished view of the gospel.

Just as the benefits of a spouse cannot be separated from the spouse himself, the benefits of salvation cannot be separated from the Son of God. It's not just his work that saves, as if he earned something on the cross that he passes off to us for our salvation. It is his very person that he came to offer us. Christ did not come to hand us his divine trophy but to carry us in his person across a finish line we could never have crossed on our own; he does not open the door to a storehouse of riches he is willing to share with us, but is *himself* the riches of heaven poured out for us. In salvation, God gives us nothing short of his very self to save us.

The Crux of Our Salvation

While we may be more familiar with other doctrines of salvation—doctrines like justification and adoption and redemption (if you're not familiar with these, don't worry: we will unpack them shortly)—they all hinge on this profound realty: Christ offers us union with himself, and that union is our salvation.

Like the center of a wagon wheel, the doctrine of union with Christ is what supports every other doctrine that encircles it. Justification is the result of our being united to the Justified One; adoption is the result of our union with the Son of God; our sanctification is the result of our being united to the Holy One. All of the gospel, the entire message of salvation, find their source and substance in this central doctrine of union with Christ.

In fact, we may come to consider these other doctrines the "benefits" of salvation. All of them are key components of our study of salvation (formally known at *soteriology*), but we find that none of them paint the entire picture we find in God's Word. But when we consider Christ himself and our union with him as our salvation, we find that all these other benefits are ours as well.

Like being united to the spouse of your deepest affections—a person whom you love and cherish, appreciate and enjoy—whose presence in your life brings all the practical benefits of marital life as well. In the same way, the believer who is united to the Son of God himself automatically receives all the benefits of salvation found in him.

Is It Biblical?

We have actually become so comfortable with dissecting the person of Christ from salvation that we must pause and ask a question: Is speaking of salvation in terms of union really biblical? Given our generations of speaking of the gospel in more didactic terms, we might wonder if we're theologically overstepping. We're familiar with talking about Christ's death and resurrection, of Christ "making a way," of his atoning sacrifice on our behalf, but we're less familiar with talking about our union with him. And so it's only necessary to wonder: Are we assuming an intimacy with the person of Christ that the Scriptures don't really teach?

When we ask this question of the Scriptures, we will find salvation is much more audacious than we would ever dare to hope. In God's Word we see that we are not just gifted something from God, but we are gifted God himself in the person of Christ. In salvation, we are included in Christ in such a way that everything that is his is ours; everything he did and earned, all the benefits of his person and work, are ours through our oneness with him. The intimacy we have with the Son of God is farther reaching than we could have imagined. In fact, I would suggest that if we were to speak of our inclusion in Christ in the same way that the Bible speaks of it, we would find ourselves feeling immodest and imprudent—*that* is how dumbfounding our salvation in Christ is.

Abiding in the Vine

We're not the only ones to think of salvation in terms of its benefits. In fact, Jesus corrects the disciples on just this point. As the disciples ask Jesus about his works and request that he show them "the way to the Father," Jesus teaches them (and us) that he is the embodiment of our salvation (John 14:1–6). As they inquire about how Jesus will give them access to the Father, it's as if Jesus stretches out his arms in self-revealing posture and says: *It's me. I am your access.*

He tells them that when they are searching for the way to the Father, they are really looking for him. When they are looking for truth, they need not search any further than the man standing in front of them. If they are seeking eternal life, they have found it: *in him.* The way, the truth, and the life aren't something Jesus offers them without offering them his very self.

As if that weren't enough, Jesus follows with this:

> *"I am the true vine, and my Father is the vine-dresser. . . . **Abide in me, and I in you.** As the branch cannot bear fruit by itself, unless it abides in the vine, neither can you, unless you abide in me. I am the vine; you are the branches. Whoever abides **in me and I in him**, he it is that bears much fruit, **for apart from me you can do nothing**. If anyone does not abide in me he is thrown away like a branch and withers; and the branches are gathered, thrown into the fire, and burned." (John 15:1, 4–6, emphasis mine)*

Have you ever seen how much space there is between a vine and its branches? Have you ever noticed the precise point where the branch stops and the vine begins?

Yeah. Me neither.

In salvation, Jesus offers union with himself to his people. Just as a branch will shrivel when disunited from its vine, so is the person apart from Christ. Jesus is emphatic: he is the source of eternal life; he is the substance of salvation. Anyone who is not *in him* will shrivel up and wither. Life is in him and there is no life apart from him.

United as His Bride

Just when we think this language might be too intimate for our polite Sunday morning theology, God's Word takes this union further. In Ephesians 5, Paul addresses the union between husbands and wives. After exhorting husbands to sacrifice and wives to submission (both of which Christ exemplifies), Paul writes this:

> *In the same way husbands should love their wives as their own bodies. He who loves his wife loves himself. For no one ever hated his own flesh, but nourishes and cherishes it, just as Christ does the church, because we are members of his body. "Therefore a man shall leave his father and mother and hold fast to his wife, and the two shall become one flesh." This mystery is profound, and I am saying that **it refers to Christ and the church.**" (Eph. 5:28–32, emphasis mine)*

Expounding on the most intimate of human relationships, Paul exhorts husbands to love their wives just as they care for their own flesh; they are to delicately tend to their wives just as they would to their own frame. Paul draws on the first one-flesh union we know and cites the words spoken in Genesis 2:24. It's worth repeating:

> *"Therefore a man shall leave his father and mother and hold fast to his wife, and the two shall become **one flesh.**" (emphasis mine)*

The one-flesh union between husband and wife is the most intimate, sacred, entangled human relational experience. It is the closest we can imagine being to another person, the most personal, intertwined relationship we can name. And then Paul zooms out to interpret the bigger picture for us. This isn't ultimately about marriage or one-flesh unions; it's about Christ and his church.

When we married, life changed for both Austin and I forever because everything that belonged to the one now belonged to the other. Austin's family was now my family, and mine was his. My meager bank account was now a joint account and legally his; any student loans one of us took out were the responsibility and financial burden of the other. Our possessions were shared, our name was shared, our home was shared. Scripture even says that our bodies belonged to one another (1 Cor. 7:4). Everything that was mine was suddenly his; everything that was his was suddenly mine.

This is the intimacy of the gospel. In union with Christ, all that is ours is Christ's, and all that is Christ's is ours. Our sin, shame, and guilt are now fully belonging to Christ—the Christ who was incarnated into our fallen form, bearing the burden of our sinful humanity and who paid the penalty for that sin on the cross. *And* all that is Christ's is ours. Christ has been united with his people in salvation and all that is his he makes ours through union: his righteousness is ours, his inheritance is ours, his Sonship is ours, his access to the Father is ours. Even his people—his holy family comprised of all those united to the Son—is suddenly and joyfully ours, as each member "belongs to all the others" (Rom. 12:5 NIV). All that is Christ's, is now fully, brazenly, rightfully ours in salvation.

This is why Paul says with astonishing confidence: "I have been crucified with Christ. It is no longer I who live, but Christ who lives in me. And the life I now live in the flesh I live by faith in the Son of God, who loved me and gave himself for me" (Gal. 2:20).

By Grace through Faith

Every believer is united to Christ in the same way Paul confessed: by faith in the Son of God. God calls us to place our faith in his Son and grants us his Spirit to dwell within us. How are we made one with the risen Lord? As we "believe in the Lord Jesus Christ" we are saved (Acts 16:31), and the Spirit of God takes up residence within us, bringing the person of Christ to bear on our lives through union with him.

Both of these points—the response of faith and the indwelling of the Spirit—require some clarification. We can't risk misspeaking about these aspects of the gospel call or we will risk losing the richness of the salvation story.

As good evangelicals, we are likely quick to affirm *sola fide* (by faith alone), but sometimes the way we speak about faith in Christ twists our faith into an exercise of work. We tend to think of our faith in Christ as if it were a merit—the righteous response of an intellectual person that makes us acceptable to God.

But the opposite is true, and we know it all too well. Our faith is faulty, flailing, and fallen. We believe and then disbelieve. If our union with the Son of God were based on our ability to believe faultlessly, we would all be condemned. What is essential is not the quality of our faith but the reliability of the One in whom our faith is put. It's the object of our faith, not the unwavering nature of our faith, that makes us acceptable to God.

Consider a child wading out into the ocean with his father. He grabs his father's hand and takes cautious steps alongside his father into the water. In the first few steps, the child may think he is holding onto his father's hand for stability and balance, but as the water grows deeper and the current pushes against his unsturdy legs, the reality is much more obvious: his grip isn't strong enough to cling to his father. His father must be the one to hold onto him.[1]

Our salvation does not rely on our ability to believe, but rests on the One in whom we believe. God doesn't look at the measure of our faith and allot us proportional salvation, as if he were counting our wages. No, our faith clings to the hand of the Faithful One. It's not our grip on Christ that will save us in the end, but his unflinching grip from which we can never be snatched—even those of feeble faith (John 10:28).

The Spirit of God in Salvation

The Spirit of God unites all believers to the person of Christ—by grace and through faith. The indwelling Spirit is none other than the Spirit of Christ. The third person of the Trinity bears witness to Christ, testifies to Christ, points to Christ, and fixes our eyes on Christ. As the Spirit of God lives within us, we are united to Christ in salvation and enjoy all the benefits of being found in him.

When we talk about the Spirit, it is easy to slip into the misguided thinking that this union is merely "spiritual." Maybe you even sighed a bit of relief when reading about this intimate union being made reality by the Spirit because, if you're perfectly honest, spiritual union seems as if it would be less real than actual union. But nothing is further from the truth. There is nothing more real than the eternal Spirit of God who has existed and reigned since before time began.

The indwelling of God's Spirit doesn't make it "as if" we were in Christ; we actually, really, vitally *are* in Christ as his Spirit lives within us. It's not just a metaphor. It is not just a word picture. All believers are in Christ by his Spirit through faith—and that is the gift of God (Eph. 2:8–9).

---

[1] Dane Calvin Ortlund, *Gentle and Lowly: The Heart of Christ for Sinners and Sufferers* (Wheaton, IL: Crossway, 2020).

All Other Doctrines Hang on This One

At this point you might be wondering if it's all too good to be true. Does it all sound too intimate, too amazing, too incredible to be your actual reality as a believer today?

If your jaw has dropped in shock and bewilderment to consider so great a salvation, then you're in good company. I don't think there is a single more life-changing truth I have ever encountered than this one.

That "all is ours in Christ" is an astounding reality in the life of the Christian. Marcus Johnson, the man who taught me about union with Christ when I was a Bible student in his Systematic Theology class, writes this about what it means to be found in Christ:

> To experience fellowship with the Son is to be made alive in Christ, justified in Christ, sanctified in Christ, seated in the heavenly realms in Christ, built up into Christ and given fullness in Christ. Those joined to Christ are "members of Christ," "crucified with Christ," "included in Christ," "baptized into Christ," and "the body of Christ." They eat and drink Christ; they are one with Christ; Christ dwells in them and they dwell in him; and they can do nothing apart from him.[2]

All other aspects of salvation rest in our union with Christ. This is why Paul writes so emphatically: "And because of him you are in Christ Jesus, who became to us wisdom from God, righteousness and sanctification and redemption . . ." (1 Cor. 1:30). Did you catch that? Christ *is* all these things to us. They are not something adjacent to him, nor can they be abstracted

---

[2] Marcus Peter Johnson, *One with Christ: An Evangelical Theology of Salvation* (Wheaton, IL: Crossway, 2013), 38–39.

from him. Justification, adoption, preservation, and glorification all find their substance in our union with Christ.

Justified in Christ

If you have ever signed a lease, enrolled in a phone plan, or checked that pesky little box that reads "I have read and agree to the terms and conditions," you have dabbled in legal language. More than that, you've entered into a legal agreement—one that has requirements and penalties, demands and promises. Your landlord promises to grant you access to your apartment in exchange for monthly rent; your phone company promises to give you data, so long as you don't default on your bills.

The doctrine of justification articulates our salvation from a legal vantage-point. God himself is the absolute moral standard, the benchmark of perfect righteousness. As such, God gets to set forth the legal terms of his creature's relationship to him. His requirement? Righteousness. The consequences for failing to meet this requirement? Death.

In the garden, Adam and Eve broke this legal requirement as they disobeyed God. The first man and woman tasted the promised consequences: they would live their lives separated from God in spiritual death, and, one day, they would physically die. Through their willful disobedience, sin entered the world, and with it, death came to all mankind. The Scriptures tell us that all humanity is incorporated "in Adam"; every person ever born inherits Adam's guilt and deserves God's judgment because of all sin (Rom. 5:12). The Bible tells us that no one is righteous—not even one (Rom. 3:10–12). Our best efforts to live righteously are, at best, filthy rags (Isa. 64:6).

God, in his perfection, cannot change the requirements and give us a pass (Luke 18:9–14). Because he is just, he cannot go back on what was decreed at the beginning of time. His requirements were broken, his demands botched. Sin left us with a need to be "made right" before God—a task that we, in and of ourselves, had no hope of accomplishing. We broke our legal relationship with God and needed to be justified—we needed a way for our sins to be forgiven and for us to be granted an undeserved righteous status before our righteous God.

Jesus, in his person and work, is our justification.

The Son of God became man in order to perfectly fulfill the righteous requirements of God's Law. Jesus not only fulfilled every Old Testament prophecy concerning himself, but he lived the sinless life that every person has failed to live. In his death on the cross, Jesus was the flawless sacrifice God's law demanded; his life was the payment the debt of our sin required. Jesus was, you could say, the perfect "contract keeper" that we all failed to be, paying the penalty for our sin and earning the righteous status we could not gain on our own.

Christ offers us a way to be pardoned of our sins and considered righteous *as we are found in him*. This is what the Reformers called the "Great Exchange"—our sins were credited to Jesus' account, and his righteousness credited to ours. By faith in Christ alone, sinners can be justified—made right before God and given confidence to stand before his righteous judgment without fear of condemnation.

How is this possible? How is it that Christ's righteousness is considered our own? How is it that our sins have been dealt with by another? Because just as we were sinful "in Adam," the audacious declaration of the gospel is that we are now declared righteous "in Christ":

> *Therefore, just as sin came into the world through one man, and death through sin, and so death spread to all men because all sinned. . . . But the free gift is not like the trespass. For if many died through one man's trespass, much more have the grace of God and the free gift by the grace of that one man Jesus Christ abounded for many. And the free gift is not like the result of that one man's sin. For the judgment*

*following one trespass brought condemnation, but
the free gift following many trespasses brought justification. (Rom. 5:12, 15–16)*

*Therefore, as one trespass led to condemnation for
all men, so one act of righteousness leads to justification and life for all men. For as by the one man's
disobedience the many were made sinners, so by the
one man's obedience the many will be made righteous. (Rom. 5:18–19)*

*For as in Adam all die, so also in Christ shall all be
made alive. (1 Cor. 15:22)*

We sinners have been justified before God because we are
united to the Righteous One. No longer do we stand before God
in our sin and shame, bearing the just consequences for breaking
God's perfect law. We now stand before God *in Christ*—bearing
the reward of his righteousness, fully justified before the righteous Judge. In Christ our sins are removed; in Christ, his righteousness is gained; in Christ, we are justified.

Adopted in Christ

Another way the Scriptures speak of our fallen state is by
calling us "children of wrath" (Eph. 2:3). Born in our sinful state,
from the womb we are deserving of God's just judgment. But
sin wasn't just our nature from birth; we lived into this nature,
willfully breaking God's commands and living as "sons of disobedience" (Eph. 2:2). Sin broke our relationship with God the
Father, leaving us without a spiritual home and without hope in
this world (Eph. 2:12).

This is why Jesus' words soothe like salve on our aching ears:
"I will not leave you as orphans; I will come to you" (John 14:18).
And he did. Jesus came, and through his person, life, death, res-
urrection, and ministry, he made a way for us to be united to him

in salvation. Through union with the Son of God, we gain adoption as sons and daughters of God.

> *To redeem those who were under the law, so that we might receive adoption as sons. And because you are sons, God has sent the Spirit of his Son into our hearts, crying, "Abba! Father!" So you are no longer a slave, but a son, and if a son, then an heir through God. (Gal. 4:5–7)*

Because we are one with the Son of God, all that is rightfully his as the Son is now ours in salvation. All who receive the Son by believing in his name have the right to be children of God—and that is what we are! (John 1:12). In Christ, we are no longer spiritually homeless; we no longer have a broken relationship with the Father. Christ's access to the Father is our access to the Father; Christ's inheritance as the Son of God is our inheritance as his children; Christ's Sonship is our sonship. We orphans are adopted as God's children because we are united to his own Son.

Sanctified in Christ

God was not content to simply declare us righteous in Christ; he also desires to make us holy in Christ. What Austin and I experienced immediately upon getting married was a functional reality: all that once belonged only to one now belonged rightfully to the other. But as we have grown in marriage over the years this reality has expanded in ways we never could have imagined.

Only eight years into marriage, we are experiencing the effects of our union in more ways that I can name. We not only finish each other's sentences and have insights as to how the other will respond to a question, but we have also instinctively picked up the phone to call each other—only to find that, without a single ring, the other is on the line, having called at the exact same time. We have bought each other the same book for Christmas, adopted each other's gestures and quirks, and grown into similar schedules and routines. Our lives were one on our wedding day, but that reality continues to unfold in new experiences of that union day-by-day.

As we are in Christ, we are transformed more and more into the likeness of the One with whom we are united. Johnson puts it well: "Sanctification is that benefit of our union with Christ in which God, through the power and presence of the Holy Spirit, delivers us from our depraved natures by transforming us into the holy image of Jesus Christ through our participation in his death and resurrection."[3]

While our righteous works do nothing to gain us salvation, our sanctification is the natural result of being united with the Holy One. To treat sanctification as an opt-in course for the spiritually mature is to miss the point of union with Christ altogether. Those who are in Christ have been united to the Perfect One, the Sun of Righteousness (Mal. 4:2). "He cannot be other than who he is to us, namely our righteousness and our holiness."[4] We are made holy—incrementally, day-by-day through the Spirit's work in our lives—because we are united to the Holy One.

Glorified in Christ

Our wedding wasn't perfect. But it was.

A small gathering of dear friends from all seasons of life gathered on the South Shore of Boston, we exchanged vows, and threw a party. Somewhere between the charcuterie and clinking glasses, dancing and laughing, hugs and well-wishes, I whispered to Austin: "I wish this could last forever."

The union Christ has with his bride, the church, has a final destination in mind. The end of all of this is the marriage feast

---

[3] Johnson, *One with Christ*, 118.
[4] Ibid.

of the Lamb. When Christ returns in glory and all the saints are raised together with Christ, the union which we now experience in part will be finally realized in full. We will be united perfectly and eternally with him in glory, and the wedding feast will never end.

Edwards captures our imagination of this day by saying,

> The end of the creation of God was to provide a spouse for his Son Jesus Christ that might enjoy him and on whom he might pour forth his love. And the end of all things in providence are to make way for the exceeding expressions of Christ's close and intimate union with, and high and glorious enjoyment of, him and to bring this to pass. And therefore the last thing and the issue of all things is the marriage of the Lamb. . . . The wedding feast is eternal; and the love and joy, the sons, entertainments and glories of the wedding never will be ended. It will be an everlasting wedding day.[5]

Our union with Christ is an "already, not yet" reality. We are "already" one with Christ today. Right now, every person who has placed their faith in Jesus Christ is one with him, and in that oneness, each is justified, adopted, and being sanctified. And still there is a fullness to our union that is "not yet"—we look to the horizon of redemptive history with great anticipation of the day when Christ will return for us and take us to be where he is.

This is what Paul is speaking of when he writes of the rich mystery: Christ in you, the hope of glory (Col. 1:27). As believers, we have a sound confidence that because we are united to Christ now, we will be united to him in eternity—not only preserved

---

[5] Jonathan Edwards, *The Works of Jonathan Edwards, Vol. 23 The "Miscellanies"* (New Haven: Yale University Press, 2004. Referenced in Johnson, *One with Christ*, 187.

from separation from God in damnation, but joyfully expectant that we will spend every moment of forever united to the Savior of our affection.

"For we await salvation from him not because he appears to us afar off, but because he makes us, ingrafted into his body, participants not only in all his benefits but also in himself."[6]

Our union with him will be full and final, and we will enjoy a glorified completeness to our oneness with Christ. We are in Christ, which gives us the very real expectation that we will follow in his footsteps beyond the grave and into eternity. Because Christ was raised, we will be raised. Because Christ is now before the Father, we will be before the Father. Because Christ is glorified, we will be glorified with him. One day, our Savior who is our very life, will appear, and we will appear with him in glory (Col. 3:4).

Worshiping the Christ of Our Union

The doctrine of union with Christ rightly makes us sit back, close our eyes, and savor the goodness of God. More than any other doctrine I can name, this truth brings me to tears in adoration before the God of our salvation.

It is good and right for us to respond this way. Let your hands slip open-faced before him. Let your mind try to contemplate the depth of his union with you—the intimacy the Savior not only desires to have with you, but currently has with you as you are united to him. Let your heart sing with relief that your sins have been transferred to him and his righteousness to you. Worship the God of your salvation with affection, tenderness, warmth, and thanksgiving.

Last year, my friend Caroline and her husband adopted a little boy. He was a few months old when he arrived in their home,

---

[6] John Calvin, et al., *Institutes of the Christian Religion* (Louisville, KY: Westminster John Knox Press, 2011), 3.2.24.

and it understandably took a little while for this child to bond with her as his mother. He wasn't a particularly cuddly baby, but she shared recently that he has started to loop his chunky little arm around her neck just about every day as they transition from the late afternoon into the evening. Since his display of affection only lasts a few minutes, she said she stops everything while her son wraps his arm around her and snuggles her neck so that she can fully savor those few minutes.

Reflecting on this she said, "I think this is what it must mean to enjoy being loved." Did you catch that? To *enjoy being loved*. As she pauses each day to savor the warmth and tenderness of his little arm on her neck, closes her eyes to the to-do lists all around her, and internally marvels at the reality that this little one is voluntarily leaning into her—that's what it means to savor the fact that you are loved by another, that they cherish you, that they want to lean into you and not away from you.

This is a glimpse of what it means to worship the God of our salvation. Though there are many places this doctrine informs and transforms our daily lives, there are few as foundational as this: enjoy being loved, Christian. In Christ, the Father adores you. He is not coolly indifferent to you; he does not merely tolerate you. You are found in the eternal Son of his delight—he *delights* in you! God is endeared toward you, deeply attached to you, is fond of you. He leans in and not away. He loves you.

Before you do anything else in response to your union with Christ, do this: enjoy being loved by Christ your Bridegroom and God your Father. Savor his tenderness toward you, praise him for his adoration of you, repeat back to him the affection he holds for you. Take time each day to stop everything, ignore the yammering to-dos of life, and relish your union with your Savior. Ready yourself for the fullness of your union with Christ in heaven by enjoying being loved by him now; consider it your daily rehearsal of eternal life.

And if your love is too cold, if your affections for God have grown tepid, then pray with David: "Restore to me the *joy* of your salvation" (Ps. 51:12, emphasis mine). Ask God to stoke the coals of affection within you so that your love imperfectly mirrors his own and so your hearts grows sensitive once against to enjoying his love for you.

It's not legalism that makes this time with him a daily habit; it's love.

Our Work and God's

When reflecting on this very doctrine, Paul instructs: "work out your own salvation with fear and trembling, for it is God who works in you both to will and to work for his good pleasure" (Phil. 2:12b–13). Our worshipful response to salvation—to being united to Christ—has both a passive and active component to it. We actively seek to live transformed lives as a result of our transformed state ("work out"), and we rest in the completed work of Christ on our behalf ("for it is God who works in you").

We see this theme repeated in John 15. When Christ taught us about our union with him by way of a vine and branch, he also gave us a command that should shape our response to the doctrine of salvation. He puts it plainly:

> *"Abide in me, and I in you. As the branch cannot bear fruit by itself, unless it abides in the vine, neither can you, unless you abide in me." (John 15:4)*

Abiding in Christ requires both our reliance on the person of Christ and our willful response; it is both a resting in Christ and a striving to enter that rest (Heb. 4:11). Rankin Wilbourne skillfully captures the dual nature of this command:

> . . . abiding is an *action*. Here is something you must choose to do. Jesus *commands* us, "Abide in me." He commands us to rest in him. Like a dog commanded to stay, we must exert ourselves not to become distracted or move away

from our Master. And Jesus makes it clear that
the amount of fruit that comes out of our lives
will be a direct result of how much (John 15:5)
or how little (v. 6) we heed his commandments.[7]

Our union with Christ leads us to leap to action when we
hear his call to abide in him. As we are saved in Christ, we have
an alert expectation that all of God's promises in Christ are true,
and our worshipful response is to deliberately walk into those
truths day-by-day. We do this every time we choose to live
according to God's kingdom economy over and against the ways
of this world. When we reject the lie that we have to prove our
worth, earn our place and chart our own course and, in exchange,
embrace the gospel reality that we bring nothing to the table
of salvation except the sin that made Christ's death necessary.
When we believe that because we are in Christ, God pulls back a
chair at his eternal table, pats the seat, and tells us there is a place
for us here. We abide in Christ when we take a sober-minded
view of our Christian lives, remembering that our chosen life-
style is to follow in the ways of Christ, even as they lead us to
taking up our crosses, enduring suffering and ridicule, because
we also know his footsteps that led into the tomb also lead us
right out of the grave.

Personal Holiness

I owe a lot of my quirks to the roommates I have had.
Chandler, my roommate freshmen year of college, passed onto me
a keen ability to fit exactly one thousand shoes in my closet and
a deep hatred of the song, "What Is Love" (which was her alarm
clock for an entire year of Sundays). Anne, my seminary roommate, taught me to call shoulder massages "shoulder squeezies,"

---

[7] Rankin Wilbourne, *Union with Christ: The Way to Know and Enjoy God*
(Colorado Springs: David C. Cook, 2018), 214–15.

which I can still be heard asking Austin for on a regular basis. Simply by living in the same space with them, I passively took on their mannerisms. We become like those we spend time with; the closer we grow in relationship and proximity to them, the more likely we are to embody their habits, quirks, and traits.

It should come as no surprise that our union with the Holy One leads to our personal holiness. More than quirks or habits, Christ, as he takes up residence within us by his Spirit, is remaking us in his image each and every day. But lest we think passivity is a proper response to Christ's sanctifying union with us ("Christ will make me like himself in his own time, I'll just sit back and enjoy the ride"), Paul reminds us that our union with Christ should lead us to deliberate, personal holiness.

Addressing those who treated their union with Christ flippantly and remained in sexual sin, Paul writes this:

> Do you not know that your bodies are members of Christ? Shall I then take the members of Christ and make them members of a prostitute? Never! Or do you not know that he who is joined to a prostitute becomes one body with her? For, as it is written, "The two will become one flesh." But he who is joined to the Lord becomes one spirit with him. Flee from sexual immorality. . . . You are not your own, for you were bought with a price. So glorify God in your body. (1 Cor. 6:15–20)

Paul conceives of the believer's union with Christ as so far reaching that for a believer to sleep with a prostitute is to unite *Christ's own members* shamelessly to a prostitute. The intimacy that Christ and his followers enjoy is so intimate that we cannot sin in our bodies and Christ remain detached or indifferent. Our bodies are not our own. We can no longer do whatever we please as we once did in the flesh. We have been united to Christ—a reality that urges us toward personal holiness.

Do you want to worship the God of your union? One, like I said before, enjoy your Bridegroom. And two, get rid of all other bedfellows. Or, put more bluntly: get sin out of your life. Resting on his righteousness in salvation, strive by the power of the Spirit to live out the holiness imparted to you. Resist temptation. Flee from sin. Willfully walk in obedience.

In other words, live like you are not just saved by the glorified Jesus, nor merely recipients of his work on your behalf, but really *united* to him. Let the truth of this gospel message sink deep into your bones such that sin is repulsive to you, the lies of the enemy fall false on your ears, and the way of the flesh is repugnant to who you are at your core. This is not an exercise of self-mustered belief; it is opening our eyes to reality.

Walk from sin and walk into the new life in Christ. Because you are, dear Christian: you are *in* Christ.

6

Bibliology: Worshiping the God of the Word

> The soul can do without everything
> except the Word of God,
> without which none at all of its
> wants are provided for.[1]
> *Martin Luther*

I grew up in a large, gregarious family that loves to laugh—with each other and at each other. That means while growing up, I had no shortage of nicknames. If you're looking for an accurate portrait of the contours of my personality each year of childhood, you need look no further than the annual Christmas letter my dad would write for friends and family. They are famous in our hometown. And the nicknames they contained, well, they'll tell you a lot about who I am.

In second grade, "Pit Bull on Red Bull" was affectionately penned on the candy cane striped stationery. Why? Because I played soccer that year, and insisted that I could play both defense and offense *at the same time*. Fast-forward to fifth grade—I broke

---

[1] Martin Luther, *Christian Liberty* (Philadelphia: Fortress Press, 1957).

my foot and three toes and still wanted to compete in the state gymnastics meet. Naturally, "Tiger Meat Wrapped in Barbed Wire"was found next to my name on the pages of that Christmas's pretty little letter.

I was no dainty child, and while there were plenty of nick-names that reassured friends and family abroad of my wide shoulders and assertive personality, the nickname that surfaced more frequently than any other was "Chatty Cathy." It was uncreative and perfectly accurate. As a child, my mom would jest that I managed to fit in my daily word count by breakfast. All the funny stories my family still tells around the dinner table about my childhood have to do with me talking at exactly the wrong time. Whether it was during a funeral or standardized testing, I liked to talk, and it didn't really seem to matter if anyone was listening.

A Chatty God

It's easy for us to think of people we know to be chatty. Maybe it's the co-worker who likes to narrate their day aloud, regardless of who is trying to work around them. Maybe it's your grandmother who never wants to end a phone conversation because she has just one more story to tell or retell. Or maybe, like me, you're the chatty one: unsure of how others keep their thoughts from spilling off their tongues.

When you and I think of God, we often don't think of him as particularly talkative. In fact, if we were to ask most people about God's communication, I imagine we would get a lot of confused looks. People might wrack their minds to think of those they know who have had particular "spiritual experiences" in which they "heard from God," but apart from those charismatic expe-riences, we don't often associate speaking with the God of the Bible.

But it's the Bible itself that reminds us that we are wrong. We are incorrect every time we think God's nature is a silent one.

We have to look no further than the sixty-six books he gave us to communicate his nature, character, will, and ways to us. The Bible itself testifies to us that God utilized a massive number of words, sixty-six books, nine different genres of writing, over forty different authors, and countless illustrations, examples, narratives, and letters to do one explicit thing: communicate with us.

God, it turns out, is quite chatty. He's vigorously communicative and he has seen fit to grant us the gift of his communication in the written Word of God.

Language Barrier

If God's chattiness surprises you, it should. As we survey the nature of God, we are reminded that he is far above and beyond us. His nature is unfathomable. His wisdom is incomprehensible and his ways are unsearchable (Rom. 11:33). He is limitless; we are limited. He is boundless; we have boundaries set by his divine hand. He is Creator; we are created creatures. He is all-powerful, all-knowing and all-present; we have the measure of power he portions to us, the amount of knowledge he assigns to us, and the singular place of presence he has given to us. Our nature and God's nature are vastly different.

But beyond the distinctions in our created nature, there's another layer to our differentiation. God is a holy God; we are sinful. At our best, we were created beings with human limitations, worshiping and walking with a boundless God. But now, this side of the Fall, we are not just a limited humanity, we are a broken humanity. And our sin-bound nature separates us from the holy God of the universe. If God were put before our fallen eyes, we would not be able to behold him—and that's not even to speak of beginning to comprehend him.

Needless to say, there was a language barrier between us and God. We could not know God, understand God, or worship God in our fallen state. And God did what only he could do: he broke the silence. God himself moved in our direction by communicating with his fallen creatures. As Horton would say, "We are not the ones who overcome our estrangement from God; he heals the breach by communicating the gospel of his Son."[2]

We couldn't, but he could—and did.

This double-separation from God reveals God's speech as the astonishing gift that it is. Matthew Smethurst puts it plainly:

> So, given that we're not only creatures of the dust but traitors against heaven's throne, the talk-ativeness of God is astounding. He would have been entirely right to leave us to ourselves, sunk in an ocean of ignorance (since we are creatures) and guilt (since we're sinners). But he didn't. He peeled back the curtain. And then opened his holy mouth.[3]

The Word of God is God's great gift of speech—it is the means by which a fallen people can hear from their faultless God. The very existence of the Bible testifies to the gospel: God bridged the gap that we could not overcome, condescended to us, and communicated his rescue plan of redemption.

Chatty before Time

God has communicated his nature to us in the Word of God—and this is a great gift of grace. But we must avoid thinking that God's speaking nature flows from his communication with *us*. Reality is, of course, the other way around. God is not speaking only because we are listening; he is not only speaking

---

[2] Michael Horton, *Pilgrim Theory: Core Doctrines for Christian Disciples* (Grand Rapids: Zondervan, 2011), 51.

[3] Matt Smethurst, *Before You Open Your Bible: Nine Heart Postures for Approaching God's Word* (Leyland, England: 10 Publishing, 2019), 18–19.

for our sake. He has been a communicative God since before we were ever spoken into being by his powerful speech.

The God who speaks to us today through his Word is the same God who was perfectly content in harmonious fellowship as the Father, Son, and Spirit. Does this feel familiar—like we are touching again on the Trinity? Good. We are—because the reality of God as Trinity impacts every part of our theology, including our Bibliology (study of the Bible). Because God is triune, he is relational; because he is relational, he is a communicative God. Communicating his nature is, after all, in his nature. Self-expression is a part of his very character.

John Webster puts it this way: "Revelation is the self-presentation of the triune God, the free work of sovereign mercy in which God wills, establishes and perfects saving fellowship with himself in which humankind comes to know, love, and fear him above all things."[4] Since the triune God of the universe is a God of communication, he has expressed himself in particular ways—through creation, through Christ, and for our purposes in this chapter, through the Bible. In the Scriptures, we have God's self-expression—a message from God about God. Since the triune God of the universe is a God of communication, he has given us the Bible that we might know him as he is.

"It Looks like You"

"I don't know how to describe it . . . it just looks like you." She said it with a smile as she leaned in for a hug goodbye and headed out my front door. I closed the door behind her, leaned against it and grinned. It was everything I wanted to hear.

For many years Austin and I hoped to be homeowners, and when the Lord gave us the opportunity to purchase our home, we savored the chance to furnish and decorate it. We picked

---

[4] John Webster, *Holy Scripture: A Dogmatic Sketch* (Current Issues in Theology; vol. 1) (Cambridge University Press, 2003), 13.

out modern dining chairs that felt just right, splurged on a solid wood dining table with mid-century legs, and collected art pieces from flea markets and thrift stores. As the pieces we purchased were assembled and the space started to come together cohesively, there was no better compliment you could give us. "It looks like you," she said. And she was right.

When we make something with care and affection, it resembles us. Like art or music or fashion or even our dining room décor, when we put our heart into it, to some extent we put our nature into it as well.

The Word of God has certain attributes that we can qualify. We talk about the Word of God being authoritative or inspired or enduring—and it is. But these are no attributes that belong to the pages of the sacred text without having first belonged to its Author. Because a loving God sought to communicate to his fallen creation, the Word looks like him. It has his attributes. It follows the contours and shapes and patterns of his character and nature. As we explore Bibliology and consider what the Word of God *is*, we'll get to know the God of the Bible even more. Put another way, a study of the communication is a study of the Communicator himself.

Self-Revelation

When I was about six years old, my uncle made my siblings and me a puppet theater. It was a simple trifolded wood frame with a center cutout for our puppet performances. My aunt sewed little purple curtains over the center opening, and made us a swath of felt puppets to create endless plots and story lines.

Over the years, we made our parents sit through more than one incoherent puppet show. Several of us would squat behind the theater and wriggle our fingers to make each character's hands animate, while one sibling stood out front to narrate the story (an attempt to fill in the narrative gaps for us inexperienced playwrights). My favorite part of every production came at the end. The narrator would announce "THE END," draw the curtains closed, and pull them dramatically back again to reveal our beaming faces where the puppets had previously been. It was our form of a final bow, and we got many unearned standing ovations.

The Word of God is his self-revelation; he communicates with us in order to reveal *himself* to us. The greatest misunderstanding we can have about the Scriptures is to think of it as an exhibit for anything other than God himself. The Scriptures pull back the curtains, if you will; but it's important that we don't miss what they reveal. We mistake God for the narrator, pointing at characters in the story and telling us about what they were like (and sharing a few good rules we should follow along the way). But the Word of God is his *self-revelation*. It means, with the aim of repeating myself, he communicates with us in order to reveal *himself* to us. The curtains are pulled back, not to reveal interesting characters or exciting plot twists; the curtains are pulled back to reveal God himself. God beams from the other side of the Scriptures, joyful to share himself with us, delighting to invite us to know him, eager for us to explore the pages of his divine self-disclosure.

The Word Is Inspired

This is the intention of the Bible: to reveal God to us. And yet, we find that it was written over hundreds of years, by several authors, and in many different settings. So how, we might wonder, can all of these words be the words of God? How do I know that what is being said here is from God himself?

Throughout history, the church has held the inspiration of Scripture as a core conviction. Specifically, Christians have always believed in what is called *verbal-plenary inspiration*.[5] *Verbal*,

---

[5] The phrase "verbal-plenary inspiration" was coined in recent years, but the concept behind it has had staying power throughout church history.

meaning "words," and *plenary*, meaning "in its entirety," is our way of professing that all of the words of Scripture are inspired by God. While the word *inspired* is used culturally to speak of people who have an idea spark or a sudden burst of ingenuity, the inspiration of Scripture speaks to the reality that God used many people, from many different cultures and backgrounds, and many different kinds of writing, to produce for us a book that speaks wholly to His person and reveals his nature to his people.

Second Timothy makes this clear: "All Scripture is breathed out by God" or, as another translation puts it, "is inspired by God" (2 Tim. 3:16 CSB). Peter reiterates this truth saying, "No prophecy was ever produced by the will of man, but men spoke from God as they were carried along by the Holy Spirit" (2 Pet. 1:21). The words of the Scriptures are the very words of God.

And yet, God did not just dictate to his people. He was not simply giving the authors of Scripture a word-for-word writing assignment.

> *Okay, John, write this down: for.*
> *Next word: God. Spelled G-O-D.*
> *Then write: so loved . . .*

God didn't mechanically inspire the Word of God, but worked organically through the authors themselves, employing their cultures and personalities, gifting them with perspectives and writing styles. God chose to reveal himself by speaking through the biblical authors "at many times and in many ways" (Heb. 1:1).

This is one of the things that makes the Word of God stand alone among spiritual writings—while other spiritual leaders like Joseph Smith and Mohamed have emphatically emphasized that

---

This phrase adequately captures what orthodox Christians have always believed about the Bible: God's authoritative inspiration of the biblical text extends to the very words of the Bible, to all parts of Scripture, and to all topics to which the Scriptures speak.

they were given word-for-word renderings of what they should write, the Christian Scriptures aren't afraid of human involvement. Our God's communication isn't soiled by human flesh; his self-communication isn't diminished when wrapped in human skin. We know because that's exactly what God did in the incarnation; the Word has already been made flesh.

"Far from suppressing human involvement, God wrapped his gospel in the swaddling cloths of human speech."[6] God called each author to participate in his divine self-revelation, and when he did, he called their whole selves—their background and culture and personality and perspectives. Only a humble, gracious God would inspire his message to his creation in such a glorious way.

The Word Is Authoritative

"Because I told you to."

We've either heard it or said it (or both). The classic parental response to the relentless question "why" is not just a pacifying response, it's an appeal to authority.

A parent can put an end to an ongoing line of questioning from a child with this simple phrase only because (or, in some cases, when) they have authority over that child. It's an appeal to the parent's position. Why should you do what you're being told to do? Because I am the one telling you to do it, and I have the authority to tell you to do it. (This is also why this line never worked on my siblings when I tried it.)

The Word of God has authority because God has authority. The Scriptures have the authority to pronounce truth and untruth, right and wrong, justice and injustice because God is its Author—it is written by the source of Truth, the only One who is perfectly right, and the just Judge of the universe. Why is it true that God opposes the proud but gives grace to the humble

---

[6] Horton, *Pilgrim Theory*, 5.

(James 4:6)? Why it is true that the righteous live by faith (Rom. 1:17)? Because God said so.

We Christians aren't the only ones to believe the authority of God's Word. In fact, Jesus himself, in his earthly ministry, revealed his own view of the Scriptures. When tempted by the devil in the wilderness, Jesus appeals to the Scriptures; when confronted by Pharisees in the temple, he quotes the Old Testament prophets. For Jesus, the Scriptures were the highest court of appeal; they have authority, and he could call upon no higher source of rebuttal than the Word of God.

If this is Jesus' view of the Scriptures, it ought to be ours as well. Our culture teaches us to squirm at any suggestion that we should submit to anyone or anything, and it certainly insists that we only submit to something after we have thoroughly tested and approved it. But Scripture is no place for that. They have authority because they are authored by God himself. Whether we test and approve them or not, the Scriptures have the final say. The Word of God is authoritative because of what it is, not because of what we make of it.

And while it is true that God need not prove himself to us in order to hold authority through his Word, he has also given us the stability of a sacred text that cannot be undone. The Bible has for generations been put under the toughest scrutiny and endured the lengthiest critiques—and yet the Bible stands above the rest in terms of credibility, even according to worldly standards. Authored by God, this book cannot be undersold, and we have found, time and again, that many literary and historic scholars who set out to disprove the authority of the Word of God have found that it soars through all tests of veracity and historicity. The Bible has authority because of what it is, and this reality has proven itself time and again through human agents.

The Word Is Preserved

I remember where I was the first time I learned that the Bible was assembled. I don't know how I had missed it, but I somehow managed to graduate from Bible school without learning how the sixty-six books of the Bible came to be considered the Scriptures, and I found myself in a seminary classroom with my jaw nearly touching the floor.

When we think about the generations that have passed between when the first words of Scripture were penned in Israel's earliest days, and the last letters that were written by Paul and John near the end of their lives, we might start to wonder: How can we be sure something didn't go awry in the process? How do we know that these are the correct sixty-six books of the Bible—that we didn't miss one of the apostle's writings or mistakenly include one of John's letters that shouldn't have been added to the canon?

The Bible was, after all, compiled over the course of generations. What started with the Old Testament Law, was added to by Joshua and the prophets to create what the Israelites, at the opening of the New Testament, considered the written Word of God. After the ascension, the apostles added their accounts of Jesus' life and ministry letters; these created the basis for our New Testament. In the years that followed, there were a handful of other books (Mark, Luke, Acts, Hebrews, and Jude), which, though not authored by apostles, were affirmed as inspired by the apostles. And, being in line with the rest of Scripture and widely affirmed by Christians as being "breathed by God," they were accepted into the canon. The early church councils[7] affirmed

---

[7] It's important to note that the church has never authoritatively closed the canon, or said, "These are the books of the Bible we will believe in." Instead, their work was to recognize the nearly universal convictions of Christians around the world. For example, the first time we see a list of the twenty-seven books of the New Testament named was in the 39th Paschal Letter of Athanasius (in AD 367), and it is the precise list of the twenty-seven New Testament books we have today. This list reflected the general

these sixty-six books as the canonical books of the Bible—and we are beneficiaries of their work. The proof is in the Bibles we hold in our hands today.

We worship a sovereign God, and his sovereignty is our assurance that the Scriptures we hold are the words he intended for us. All along, God has been playing the long game; he is telling a long story, working throughout each generation and era to pen and preserve his words for his people. Because God upholds all things by the word of his power (Heb. 1:3), we can read our Bibles with confidence, and can say with the psalmist: "The words of the LORD are pure words . . . You, O LORD, will keep them" (Ps. 12:6–7).

Worshiping the Author of Scripture

If the Bible is God's self-revelation—his communication to us of who he is and what he is like—then every time we open our Bibles, we have the opportunity to worship him. Our approach to Scripture reveals our heart's posture toward the Author of God's Word. Do we believe it has the right to give us commands? Do we submit ourselves to what it says, even when it rubs us the wrong way? Do we approach it skeptically, wondering if it really has relevance to us in the twenty-first century? Do we consider it worth our time and effort to understand the cultural background a certain book was written in?

How we answer these questions says more about us than our Bible study preferences and methods. It does not just tell us

---

convictions of Christians in the eastern part of the Mediterranean world in that day. Nearly simultaneously, the Council of Carthage, representing the churches in the western part of the Mediterranean world, were found in unison with the eastern churches: their estimation of the New Testament canonical books was precisely the same. The way these two lists came about reminds us that God is the one identifying for his people which books of the Bible were breathed out by him.

what we make of the Scriptures; it tells us what we make of God himself.

If we believe that the Bible is God's divine self-expression—his words about himself for his people—we will find ourselves approaching our study of Scripture differently as a result. Knowing that these pages gift us the opportunity to know God, we will read them eagerly, not apathetically. We will read them submissively, not skeptically. We will read them confidently, not anxiously. Recognizing what the Bible *is* will transform our approach to this holy text and will throw us headlong into worshiping the God who inspired his Word, embedded it with authority, and preserved it through the ages.

A Story-Telling People

Have you ever thought about the one big story of the Bible? The metanarrative (meta, meaning *big*, and narrative, meaning *story*) of Scripture is the overarching, grand story that God is telling from Genesis to Revelation.

It was in kindness that God gave us the Scriptures as a metanarrative—a story. Regardless of culture or time or place, all humans are drawn to stories. We learn better when we learn in story form, and we relate to each other and to history best through narrative. Instead of giving us a science textbook that required a PhD to decipher, God gave us a story. Rather than giving us a codex that only the brightest minds could decode, God gave us a narrative. When God chose to reveal his self to us, he told us a story—a story of a lost people and his cosmic plan to save them.

In line with the character we've seen time and time again, God condescends to his people. He isn't too polished to communicate with us in a story; he isn't too proper to speak to us in true tales. God our Father wasn't too important to sit down on the floor with his children and speak in hushed tones to them in ways they could understand, in a voice that brings comfort and offers peace. Having formed us to be a story-telling people, he wrote us a grand story to tell us all about who he is—to put his nature and character on display for us.

Calvin beautifully captures this humility of God: "For who even of slight intelligence does not understand that, as nurses commonly do with infants, God is wont in measure to 'lisp' in speaking to us? Thus such forms of speaking do not so much express clearly what God is like as accommodate the knowledge of him to our slight capacity. To do this he must descend far beneath his loftiness."[8]

This isn't inconsequential for us as modern Christians. It's imperative that we remember that the Bible isn't a catalog of moralistic heroes we should emulate (in fact, it hosts some messy characters we'd likely rather not be associated with). It isn't an apologetic for a particular political position or the newspaper in advance. It is ultimately a story. And just when we think we're too respectable to be told tales or too scholarly to believe in stories, we're reminded that sometimes stories are true. (In fact, the best ones always are.)

The Hero of the Story

Though the Bible comprises thousands of smaller stories with their own characters and teaching, when considered all together we find that God is telling one grand story on every single page. And it's the story about his Son.

I love how Sally Lloyd-Jones puts it in her children's Bible. She says, "every page whispers his name."[9] It's absolutely true. Every single page of Scripture is written to bear witness to the Son of God who came to save God's people from their sin and

---

[8] John Calvin, et al., *Institutes of the Christian Religion* (Louisville, KY: Westminster John Knox Press, 2011), 1.13.1.

[9] Sally Lloyd-Jones, *The Jesus Storybook Bible: Every Story Whispers His Name* (Grand Rapids: ZonderKidz, 2007).

make them right with God again. The Old Testament anticipates him as the promised Savior, and the New Testament proclaims that he has come—God has kept his promises. Jesus himself emphasizes this to his disciples; appearing to them after the resurrection, he says, "everything written about me in the Law of Moses and the Prophets and the Psalms must be fulfilled" (Luke 24:44). And the text tells us that "beginning with Moses and all the Prophets, he interpreted to them in all the Scriptures the things concerning himself" (Luke 24:27). From Genesis when God promised the newly fallen man and woman that One would come to crush the deceiving serpent's head, to the book of Revelation when God glorifies the One who defeated death, the Bible's overarching story points us directly to the person and work of Jesus Christ.

The biggest mistake we can make in reading the Bible is to assume it's a story about us. When we search the Scriptures for steps to self-help or anecdotes for self actualization, we will find ourselves massively disappointed. That's not what the Scriptures are for. They are a grand narrative of God's salvation plan, and we are not the hero of that story.

The grand story of the Bible tells us that all mankind needed a Savior to make us right with God. The hero of the story—the narrative's pinnacle and climax and lynchpin—is Jesus. This is *why* every page whispers his name: it is the name we must hear, for there is no other name by which we can be saved (Acts 4:12). It's no wonder we have learned to shrug our shoulders indifferently at the notion of daily Bible study when we have for so long looked to them to tell us a story about ourselves. That would be a bland, boring story and one that anyone should easily tire of. But that's not what the Bible is. The Bible is not a human self-help book; it is God's majestic self-revelation, his merciful unveiling of a redemption plan that hinges on him sending his Son. It's a marvelous story—not only because it has a divine hero, but because it's true.

Yes, the Bible tells us one grand story. What's more? It's a true, living and breathing story that has bearing on our lives today *because it testifies to Christ*. Because it points us to the living Savior who wants to redeem us, it works on every one who reads it. It's "living and active" (Heb. 4:12). The Word of God is dynamic and real. The story of redemption jumps off the pages of the sacred, ancient text and changes our lives today in real-time.

Jesus himself makes this point so strongly that he confronts the religious elite saying, "You search the Scriptures because you think that in them you have eternal life; it is they that bear witness about me" (John 5:39). Jesus' point is this: you can read the Scriptures all you want, but they lie fallow in your hearts until we recognize the Savior in their pages. The Scriptures, in a sense, are useless to us unless we recognize ourselves in the pages of the Word—seeing our sinfulness, our separation from God and our need for a Savior—and seeing Jesus Christ as the Savior we desperately need.

Jesus makes the Story what it is. Jesus Christ makes Scriptures the witness that they are. It's Jesus who brings the metanarrative of Scripture into living color, real-life action, and helps it find its feet in the everyday life of everyday men and women.

Living Story

For many years, I was a Bible student. I mean an actual Bible student—in Bible school, writing Bible papers and learning the biblical text. But even as immersed as I was in text, I missed something for years. I thought I was studying the Bible, but I didn't realize it was actually studying me.

The author of Hebrews makes a point to say that the Word of God is alive—a notion with which we're all likely familiar and comfortable. But then they go on to say this:

> *[The Bible is] sharper than any two-edged sword,*
> *piercing to the division of soul and of spirit, of joints*

and of marrow, and discerning the thoughts and
intentions of the heart. (Heb. 4:12)

The Bible works on us as we work on it. Like a sharp blade, it
slices through us and it perceives every hidden area of our thinking or purpose. When we read the Word, nothing is hidden from
God's view. The Scriptures study us as we study it; it reads us as
we read it.

When we come to God's Word, we can expect more than we
would in reading any other book—this book is alive! It is going
to splay out our hearts' contents before the Lord; it is going to
change us simply for having read the living words therein.

The Law of Life

We might, then, start to wonder what all of the Old
Testament books are for. After all, have you read Exodus and
Leviticus? There's an exciting story about a sea that parted at
the beginning, and after that . . . just a bunch of laws. We might
wonder how the Law of God throughout the Old Testament fits
into the "living and active" Word presented to us on the pages of
the New Testament.

The Law God gave his people was a list of rules and regula-
tions for them to follow, but they were also more than that. They
were an invitation to his people to mirror his character. Since
his people had fallen away from him in sin, they had no hope of
being like God. And so, God graciously gives them the Law. In
it, he outlines for them the way he would have his people live.
He would have them govern justly because he is a just God; he
would have them tithe because he is a generous God; he would
have them observe the sabbath because he himself is a God of
rest.

But God knew something that even Israel often failed to
recognize: they would never be able to accept God's invitation
to reflect his character. Though the invitation itself was a mercy

from God, they would fail him at every turn. And that was exactly the point.

The Law of God was given to his people to reveal their deep need for him, to remind them that they couldn't keep his commands, even on their best days. The Old Testament books stood as testimonies to God's people: you cannot be righteous on your own. You need a Savior.

The Law of God—yes, even those long books of measurements and descriptions of feasts and fasts—were living words that worked on the people of God. They pointed to their need for a Savior and reminded them at every turn: the Savior is on his way.

An Equipping Word

So why don't we just sit back and read our Bibles all day? Why don't we just let it do its work without bothering with the stuff of service, mission, and church life?

Paul answers this question in his letter to Timothy. As the young pastor sought to shepherd a church of new believers, Paul writes to him and says:

> *All Scripture is breathed out by God and profitable for teaching, for reproof, for correction, and for training in righteousness, that the man of God may be complete, **equipped for every good work**. (2 Tim. 3:16–17, emphasis added)*

The purpose of the Scriptures is more than just head knowledge. They change us and make us more like the Author. As the Word of God works on us, it teaches us. That means it instructs, tutors, and coaches us in the way that we should go so that we learn to walk the road of Christlikeness. It also reproves us: when our feet stray and our hearts go wayward, the Bible offers a rebuke, disapproving of that which is our detriment. The

Scriptures correct us, meaning they show us true north when we are wandering from God, putting our feet again on the path of sanctification (Psalm 119:105). And the Word trains us: exercising and coaching us that we might look more like the God it proclaims.

But that's not all the Word does. Moving beyond personal holiness, the Scriptures propel us into service and mission! As the Bible does its work on us by the Spirit, it supplies us with everything we need to live out the call of Christ on our lives. In the pages of God's Word we are compelled to join in the work of God in the world, driven to be a part of sharing the good news of the gospel—the hope we ourselves have found therein.

> Christians don't simply learn or study or use Scripture; we assimilate it, take it into our lives in such a way that it gets metabolized into acts of love, cups of cold water, missions into all the world, healing and evangelism and justice in Jesus' name, hands raised in adoration of the Father, feet washed in company with the Son.[10]

Everything for Faith and Practice

We can't help but notice that this verse uses the word *every* when referring to the extent to which the Word equips us for good work. *Every good work?*, you might be wondering? Then why don't I find the Scriptures speaking to every question I have? Why don't they answer all of my modern dilemmas about how to live out the Christian life?

Have you ever wished the Bible spoke to some of your current, contextual questions about Christian living? I have often

---

[10] Eugene H. Peterson, *Eat This Book: A Conversation in the Art of Spiritual Reading* (Grand Rapids: William B. Eerdmans Publishing Company, 2006), 18.

wanted it to tell me exactly what kind of movies were okay for believers to watch, what kind of schooling to choose for my children, or how to spend my paycheck each month. When we look to the Bible to answer our every modern question, we'll often find ourselves frustrated, and we'll be much more prone to taking a verse out of context or reading something in a passage that isn't really there.

Underneath this desire to have the Bible speak to every question we have is a bend toward legalism. I want God to give me a rule for every area of life; that way, I can obey and be assured that I am pleasing God. But this verse reminds us that the Word is an equipping Word; its task is to not just give us the right answers to every question, but to transform us into the right kind of people. The way it works on us as we read it is that it makes us more like God—teaching us to think his thoughts, love his loves, hate his hates, value his values. It changes us into people who are, at root-level, more like Christ.

The Word of God by the Spirit will give us everything we need for faith and practice, even if it does not answer all of our questions on Christian living. In the pages of Scripture we will find commands and principles to abide by (and we should), but as it works on us it will also make us into people who discern what is best (Phil. 1:10). It will teach us the wisdom to know what to put before our eyes; it will communicate to us the heart of God for his children; it will equip us with generosity and insight on how to rightly allocate our resources.

What's It Worth?

Do you remember the old PBS show *Antiques Roadshow*? I'm sure I'm dating myself with this reference, but it was a favorite of mine as a kid. I loved seeing people bring their vintage collection or garage sale finds to experts to find out the worth of their antiques. Sometimes they would be surprised to find out their $5 bargain was worth thousands; more often than not, they would walk away disappointed because their great-grandmother's heir-loom was only worth a few bucks.

Knowing what something is worth enables us to treat it properly. When we know that the coffee table we inherited is worth thousands, we are less likely to leave it in the garage and more prone to reach for a coaster. Once we know the value of an item, we can assign it proper worth in our perspective and approach.

This is the essence of worship: assigning worth to some-one or something. The trick is to assign worth where it actually exists, which is why the only One worthy of our worship is the God of the Bible. We worship God when we ascribe him the worth due to his name; when we recognize his worthiness, we approach him—and his Word—with the proper affection, awe, and adoration.

Too Intimidating? Or Too Familiar?

I have spent many years of ministry trying to help believ-ers overcome their intimidation of the Scriptures. I had read the statistics (and observed it in my own local church context) about how few Christians spent daily time in the Word. So, I taught workshops and wrote lessons with one primary aim: to make the Bible approachable to everyday Christians.

But I'll be very honest here: I was surprised to find far fewer believers than I anticipated were intimidated by their Bibles. Though I assumed that this was the primary factor keeping believers from daily time in the Word, not many Christians I was reaching were daunted by the idea of studying the Bible. What was I missing? Why were so many believers out of the habit of studying the Word regularly?

The problem I encountered in my circles of the church was not unfamiliarity with Scripture, but over-familiarity. It wasn't that they were uncertain as to how to approach the Bible; it's that they had heard parts of it so many times that it had lost its appeal. While many had come to Christ at a young age and eagerly devoured Scripture early in life, they had grown tired of the habit, unsure as to whether or not it was worth getting up early in the morning or making time during the day to spend time reading the words they had grown so accustomed to hearing.

They are not alone. I join their ranks as a Christian who has often shrugged my shoulders dismissively at studying the Word simply because I have let it become commonplace in my mind and routine. I have let my daily quiet time become a burden because I have approached the Word of God as if it were an ordinary, routine, average book on my to-read list. I have not accredited it with proper worth—worth that it inherently holds—and have failed to worship the God of the Bible as a result.

How to Approach Your Bible

Having seen what the Bible is and what it does should change how we approach it. In fact, I'd suggest that our worship is found in our approach to the Word of God even more so than it is in how much time we read or what we read in any given day. Our heart posture before we even crack open the cover is going to set the tone for our study of Scripture and our worship of its Author.[11]

Approach Your Bible with Delight

The Word of God is God's self-revelation, and in it condescends to communicate his nature to us. We are not entitled to our Bibles; we do not deserve to know who God is or what he is like. This is a privilege that we enjoy exclusively because he is a kind Father who delights in stooping down to our level, in our language, in order to share his good self with us.

---

[11] For this portion, I am deeply influenced by the great work of Matthew Smethurst in his little book on heart postures for reading your Bible. Matt Smethurst, *Before You Open Your Bible: Nine Heart Postures for Approaching God's Word* (Leyland, England: 10 Publishing, 2019).

Our drudgery over the Word can often be traced back to entitlement. Particularly in our Western culture with an abundance of Bibles and translations at our fingertips, we are more prone to think that we deserve God's Word—in fact, we have felt this way for so long that reading the Word has become a burden, a hard item on our daily to-do list. But God's self-revelation reminds us that we could not overcome the language barrier that existed between us and God; he had to do it. And he did.

In response, we should approach our Bibles with all the hunger and craving of a parched marathon runner who cannot gulp it down fast enough. God has opened to us a means of knowing him; he has communicated his very nature to us in a way that we can understand. The God of our affection, the King of our salvation, the Hero of the redemption story is telling us what he is like and inviting us to mirror his own character. In the pages of Scripture, we are invited to sink deeper into friendship with God, getting to know him better each time we open the book.

Knowing that this worth—the value of knowing God more—lies within the pages of our Bible should cause our hearts to burst with joy. Like the prophet Jeremiah, we will say:

> *Your words were found, and I ate them, and your words became to me a joy and the delight of my heart, for I am called by your name, O LORD, God of hosts. (Jer. 15:16)*

As this truth settles into our minds and postures, we will find our hearts swelling with delight to dive into the Bible and know him more each day. We will read his promises with pleasure, we will consider his commands with gladness, and we will hear the stories of old again and again with hearts full of rejoicing precisely because it is a delight to know our God.

Approach Your Bible Thoughtfully

Does the technical part of the conversation about the Word's inspiration and preservation feel dry to you? Do you wonder how it can lead you to worship?

I have often asked the same question. But through my time in the seminary classroom studying the different human authors of the Word and how the Lord has preserved his Word throughout church history, I have seen how much these insights influence our approach to Scripture.

Because God saw fit to use different human authors to write his Word, because he didn't consider the cultural backgrounds of his authors to sully his communication, and because he preserved his Word over the long-haul as it was written and assembled, we must approach our Bibles thoughtfully.

When asked which was the greatest command in the Law, Jesus responded: "love the LORD your God with all your heart and with all your soul and with all your mind" (Matt. 22:37). While many of us are likely familiar with love that pours from our hearts and souls, we don't often think of love gushing forth from our minds. Maybe even especially when it comes to worship, when we think of pouring out our love for God, our minds are not often the first source we think of.

But because God, in his sovereignty, gave us his Word written in many different time periods, cultures, places and genres, we must approach our Bibles as students. We must be willing to do the hard work of learning the cultural background that a given book is written to. Why? Because it will help us better understand how God is communicating to us. We should be eager to do the intellectual work of recognizing different biblical genres—how come? Because we serve a God who chose to communicate to us through poetry and narrative and prophecy, and we don't want to think these choices inconsequential.

Approach Your Bible with Desperation

Final words are important. We give them more weight because, more often than not, the person speaking them chooses them with more care. After leading the nation of Israel for years, Moses speaks to God's people one final time. He relays to them everything God is commanding and calling them to, and then he concludes with this: "They are not meaningless words to you but they are your life" (Deut. 32:47 csb).

Not an accessory for good living. Not a supplement to being God's people. These words were their very life-source, the breath in their spiritual lungs, the blood coursing through the veins of their identity as the people of God.

Jesus puts equal stress on the Word. When countering the devil's temptation to create bread and break his fast, Jesus says this: "Man shall not live by bread alone, but by every word that comes from the mouth of God" (Matt. 4:4).

Not an appetizer to provoke our spiritual cravings. Not a snack to tide us over until something better is served. Not a dessert that caps off an otherwise righteous life. Our daily bread, everyday sustenance, the nourishment of our souls.

It's typical (and good!) for us as Christians to desire to know God the Father, to enjoy life in the Son, and to savor the fellowship of the Spirit. Yet we would know nothing of this triune God, the transformative power of his gospel, or the compelling mission of his church without his Word. The Bible is the place where God has seen fit to teach us about these things (or, for the sake of redundancy, to reveal himself to us). We show our foolishness when we claim to desire the One that Scripture proclaims without fostering a desire to read our Bibles. On the contrary, our eagerness to know God should drive us deep into the pages of Scripture.

We need God's Word. We were not created to live without it. God has gone the distance to grant us the ability to know who he is and what he is like, and he has communicated this in

Scripture. So we must approach our Bibles with eagerness and urgency. Knowing God in his Word can't wait! We need to know him, be changed by him, be drawn closer to him today—it is our very life. Approach your Bible desperately; not because you should, but because you are.

Approach Your Bible with Anticipation

I ran track when I was in junior high. I was very bad at it.

Since I went to a small school, everyone who tried out for track made the team. I'm pretty sure the coaches (comprised of a fifth grade English teacher and an eighth grade science teacher . . . you know, the pros) were just happy to have enough names to fill the rosters. So when my name appeared on several of the sprint events, it wasn't because I was any good. It was simply because I could put one foot in front of the other.

My problem wasn't with my actual run or speed; I was actually rather fast. The problem was in my starting position. Every time I would step out onto the track and find my lane, I would fidget with the starting blocks. Never able to get quite comfortable, I was never in a ready position when the starting gun rang, and my race always suffered for it.

Because the Bible is "alive and active," because it works on us, we can approach our Bibles with anticipation that it will change us. We can expect the Word of God to work in our lives in the ways that he promises it will. Here are just a few of the things that God promises his words will do in the lives of his children:

Encourage us and give us hope:

For whatever was written in former days was written for our instruction, that through endurance and through the encouragement of the Scriptures we might have hope. (Rom. 15:4)

Build our faith:

So faith comes from hearing, and hearing through the word of Christ. (Rom. 10:17)

Light our way:

Your word is a lamp to my feet and a light to my path. (Ps. 119:105)

Make us like Christ:

"Sanctify them in the truth; your word is truth." (John 17:17)

Revive our souls, make us wise, cause us to rejoice, and enlighten us:

The law of the LORD is perfect,
*   reviving the soul;*
the testimony of the LORD is sure,
*   making wise the simple;*
the precepts of the LORD are right,
*   rejoicing the heart;*
the commandment of the LORD is pure,
*   enlightening the eyes.*
(Ps. 19:7–8)

God has promised that his Word will work on us by his Spirit as we meditate on, study, and delight in his Word, which means that we can come to the Scriptures in the ready position—ready to see him work, fully anticipating that he will bear fruit in our lives. We can plant our feet firmly on the starter blocks, confident that we are going to be changed as we commune with God in the Bible.

We don't have to worry that the Word won't live up to our expectations of it; the all-powerful God of the universe authored it and gives it life and authority. It's going to do what he says it will do. It's going to change us.

Approach Your Bible Obediently

I didn't understand James 1:22–24 until I was a new mom. Speaking about those who read the Word and neglect to obey the Word, James writes this:

> But be doers of the word, and not hearers only, deceiving yourselves. For if anyone is a hearer of the word and not a doer, he is like a man who looks intently at his natural face in a mirror. For he looks at himself and goes away and at once forgets what he was like.

In the early days of my daughter's life, there were many times I looked in the mirror and walked away with zero awareness of what I was wearing or if I had any makeup on. My sleep-deprived brain was a blur and my memory was shot.

But even though this can happen in extreme circumstances (there's a reason sleep deprivation is a form of torture), it should never be the norm. If, when my daughter is three years old, I still can't recall my appearance after looking in the mirror, we would rightly conclude that something is wrong. My mind is not working the way it's designed to.

Unfortunately, this is how many of us approach the Word of God. We read it, study it, and consider it . . . and then go about our days as if the words we just read have no bearing on our behavior, thoughts, actions, or hearts. In our post-enlightenment culture, we are prone to finding the Word interesting more than we find it imposing; something for our consideration, but not for our conviction—and that is to our detriment.

God's desire is to conform us into the image of his Son, and to do that, in part, by the reading of his Word. We worship God when we consider his Word worthy of our obedience. When we recognize the authority Scripture has in our own lives and submit ourselves to it, we ascribe to God the worth he is due, granting him the proper place of authority over us.

And here's the good news: when we obey God in his Word, we set ourselves in tune with God's plan for our flourishing. Or, as pastor-theologian Eugene Peterson puts it, we "go with the grain of the universe."[12] God's commands are not arbitrary rules, tests to see if we will honor God by saying no to a better or more fulfilling life we would otherwise have. No, God has given us a pattern of life that gives him glory and satisfies the deepest desires of our hearts. We approach our Bibles obediently knowing that therein lie the good desires of our kind Father.

A Guarantee

We all have busy agendas and important things vying for our time and attention. To say, "I'm busy," these days is a non-starter. Everyone is busy. Even if they're not as busy as another, everyone feels busy because we all have multiple tasks and time lines we balance, roles, responsibilities and relationships to navigate.

One of the most important decisions we face each day is how we will spend our time. Knowing where to invest our 24 hours, 1,440 minutes, 86,400 seconds each spin of the globe is a daunting task—especially when everyone and everything wants just a bit more of your attention.

It can be hard to know where to invest our time and make it count, which is why I'm always grateful for God's assurance in Isaiah 55:

> "For as the rain and the snow come down from heaven
>   and do not return there but water the earth,
>   making it bring forth and sprout,

[12] Eugene Peterson, *Long Obedience in the Same Direction* (Downers Grove, IL: InterVarsity Press, 2000), 121.

giving seed to the sower and bread to the eater,
so shall my word be that goes out from my mouth;
it shall not return to me empty,
but it shall accomplish that which I purpose,
and shall succeed in the thing for which I sent it."
(vv. 10–11)

Just like the hydration system of the natural world is designed such that the rain cannot hit the ground without giving it nourishment, so God's words do not hit our ears without it accomplishing his will. God sends forth his Word in power and promise—it will accomplish what he sends it to do. His words will strengthen the weak (Prov. 3:8), protect the spiritually vulnerable (Eph. 6:17), give wisdom to the wanting (Ps. 19:7), comfort the afflicted (Ps. 119:50), and guide us in the way of life (Josh. 1:8). *His words will not fail. They will succeed in the thing for which he sent it.*

Want to be sure you're investing your time in the right place? Want a guarantee that you're not wasting your time? Spend time in the Word. It will never return void. It will never turn up empty. It will always accomplish his purposes. That's God's promise to you and me.

Ecclesiology: Worshiping the God of His Body

There is no such thing as an
independent Christian.[1]

Rosaria Butterfield

I slammed the bedroom door as hard as my eight-year-old muscles could afford. The loud bang rang through the house and, in my mind, punctuated my argument perfectly.

"You are the meanest mom!" I yelled at the back of the door—one part hoping my mom would never hear me, the other part knowing that she would. I threw myself onto my teal and purple bedspread, and sobbed.

I don't remember the reason for the argument—was there a sleepover I wasn't allowed to go to? A TV show I couldn't watch? A snack I wanted but she insisted I wait for supper? Who knows.

Within a few minutes my dad came up to my room. He wasn't involved in the argument downstairs, but he was there to

---

[1] Rosaria Butterfield, *The Secret Thoughts of an Unlikely Convert: An English Professor's Journey into Christian Faith* (Pittsburgh, PA: Crown & Covenant Publications, 2014), 38.

help make it right. He pulled a chair to the side of my bed, and sat his large, former-football-player self on it. He didn't say a word, but waited for me to vent my frustration, which of course I did. I told him how mean my mom was, how there had never been another mom so horrible in all the world. I told him she was wrong, unkind, and bad (the biggest insult an elementary-age child can devise for a parent). I listed all the faults my eight-year-old self could think of, and when I ran out of breath, he took my face in his hands and held it close to his. In a gentle tone of firm resolve he whispered his rebuke: "That's my bride you're talking about."

That was one of my earliest memories of my dad chiding me or my siblings with this phrase, but it does not stand alone. When I would throw a high school tantrum in the kitchen, yelling at my mom across the kitchen island, he would gracefully place his hands on the countertop, letting his arms loom on either side of me. His face still inches overhead, he would whisper, "That's my bride you're talking about."

Now don't get the picture wrong: my mom was not the disciplinarian and my father the mediator. Both played integral roles in my discipline and upbringing, but whenever our anger or frustration turned against my mother, he was there with his signature reprimand: That's my bride.

My dad needn't say anything else, did he? That one short phrase held within its grasp the fullness of his affection for his wife, the bride of his youth, the prize of his family, the love of his life. We were allowed to be frustrated, but we would not be permitted to insult his wife; we could voice our disagreement, but we would not be allowed to make her the target of our anger.

What the Church Can Be

When we think about the church, for many of us who have been churched for the better part of our lives, our thoughts generally circle around this sentiment: the church is messy and hard, but important. We might even dare to say the church is messy and hard, but good. But whatever positive attribute we put at the end of that phrase, the first two words are almost always the same: the church is messy and hard.

I am not one to pretend that church hurt isn't real. It is, and it is woefully painful. In fact, for many of us the pain the church has caused in our personal lives is so great that turning the page to this chapter title made your heart beat a little faster, and forced a deep breath inside your chest.

I, too, have known several seasons of deep hurt within the church. I have found myself much more able to name her flaws than her joys—much more ready to point out her deficiencies than her distinct qualities. I could easily tell you that the church is broken, fallen, sinful, and hypocritical. But in those moments of hurt, anger, and frustration, I hear the Spirit of Christ's voice come in close and whisper, "That's My bride you're talking about."

Have you ever noticed that for all of the church's flaws—and God knew she would have them—the Bible doesn't paint an irritated view of the church? When we look at the pages of God's Word, we see a portrait of his bride that might surprise our wounded hearts. In fact, we might read the words God speaks about the church and struggle to believe they are true. Because, in the Bible, God so closely relates to his church, holds her with such esteem and affection, that he leaves for us a mysterious, dynamic, powerful picture of what it means to be his.

And so, I want to ask us to do something brave in this chapter. I want to invite us to catch God's vision for the church, to see her as he sees her, to stoke the coals of affection in our hearts as we read of his great love for her. I want us to momentarily lay aside our experiences in the church in order to gain theological perspective. For the next several pages this is my invitation to you: look to God's Word and see what the church *can* be.

What Is the Church?

The Bible holds out a beautiful portrait of what the church can be, and before we look at the word-pictures that underpin our theological reality, it's important to first ask the question: Who is it that we're talking about? Who is the church?

Here is a helpful working definition: the church is the gathering of those who have been reconciled to the Father through Jesus, have been united to him in faith and thereby united to each other, and through his indwelling Spirit, bring God's presence to bear in the world; this gathering also practices the Lord's ordinances together and its members enjoy covenantal commitment to one another, being under the authority of spiritual shepherds and delighting in the headship of Christ, its Good Shepherd. First, and perhaps most important, the church is a people, not a place. Do you remember the nursery rhyme and accompanying hand motions? "Here is the church, here is the steeple. Open the door and see all the people." Not to put it too harshly, but . . . no. The church is not the building she meets in, but the body that gathers; not the worship space she occupies, but the worshipers therein; not a facility, but a family.

God didn't create for himself an organization or a non-profit. He created a people—those who are called out of their human identities, and are given new identities as his own; those who are called out of their human cultures, and are called to live according to God's ways. God wasn't in the business of creating a network or a blog or podcast or committee. He has always been after the people.

God's People

Secondly, we can't help but notice that God's vision for his people is both singular and plural. When speaking about his church, he says this:

*But you are a chosen race, a royal priesthood, a holy
nation, a people for his own possession, that you may
proclaim the excellencies of him who called you out
of darkness into his marvelous light. (1 Pet. 2:9)*

I've never known a single-person race, a priesthood consisting of only one priest, a people consisting of only one person.
Nowhere in the Scriptures are we given the sense that we are
ever "doing church" on our own; that when we're at home in our
PJs on a Sunday morning with our Bible open that what is happening is of the same quality and content as what is happening
in the corporate lives of believers. God's desire for his church
is for a multiplicity of individuals to create a unified whole; or,
from many people (plural) to create a new people (singular). In
creating his church, God made her to be more than the sum of
her parts. He calls individuals into saving union with his Son, he
ushers them into the corporate life of his church and makes them
something distinct.

This might be harder for our individualistic Western minds
than it is for others to grasp. God saves sinners and immediately
includes them in the congregation of the saved. This is why historic theologians were right when they insisted that there is no
salvation apart from the church. What they were *not* saying is
that individuals in the church are the ones handing out salvation; what they *did* mean is that there is no way for someone to
be saved without becoming a part of God's people, the church.
Put another way, there's no way to be united to the Son without
also being united to everyone else who is united him—meaning,
his people. Cyprian of Carthage put it in a snarky manner: "He
cannot have God as a father who does not have the Church as a
mother."[2]

---

[2] Saint Cyprian, "The Unity of the Church," *Treatises (The Fathers of
the Church, Volume 36)*, trans. Roy J. Deferrari (Washington, DC: Catholic
University of America Press, 2010), 100.

Since the beginning, God has been making for himself a beloved people—a gathering of those who are saved by faith and filled with his Spirit, thereby bringing his presence to bear in this world. Because of this, the church should never be seen as a side bonus of our salvation. It's not the optional extra, like guacamole on your burrito bowl. It is not what you do, Christian; it is *who you are*. You, together with every other individual found in Christ by grace and faith, are a member of his bride, his body, and his flock.

The Church, His Bride

Before the Scriptures even use the term "church," we find God reaching toward his people in saving relationship. This relationship, in biblical terms, is called a *covenant*. Knowing that his people are fallen and cannot reach out toward him, God extends himself toward his people in grace and mercy. And God not only desired to save his people from their sin, but to make them his own; he would not simply settle for rescuing them from drowning in the sea of their sin and dropping them at the nearest safe shoreline. No. He wanted to marry them.

Isaiah, speaking prophetically for God, captures God's heart:

> *For your Maker is your husband,*
> *   the LORD of hosts is his name;*
> *and the Holy One of Israel is your Redeemer,*
> *   the God of the whole earth he is called.*
> *(Isa. 54:5)*

In Isaiah's day, it would have been one thing to be a Maker. A maker, naturally, owns the thing he creates; because it came from his own mind and was created by the work of his own hands, the object created was the maker's possession. It would have been another thing to be a redeemer. When someone paid the debt another owed and gave them their freedom, they became their

Redeemer—one deserving of gratitude, esteem, and service in return.

But that's not the punch line of Isaiah's prophecy. God wants his people to know that their Maker is their *Husband*—the one who created you wants more than ownership. He wants affectionate relationship with you. God wants more than just to redeem his people; he doesn't just want to be deserving of their honor and service. He is their husband.

Have you ever known a couple who are so infatuated with each other that they are contemplating marriage? I remember one passing conversation in Bible school. "We've never had a fight or even a disagreement, so I'm thinking he might be the one." We all know those who have been so enamored with each other that they overlook the other's flaws. But this is not how it is with God. God is not under any delusions. God doesn't desire to make the church his own because he finds her faultless; in fact, he knows better than we ever will the depths of her darkness and the lengths to which she will go to break their covenant relationship. If anyone has endured church hurt, it is God.

That is why the covenant between God and his people rests on God's character, not ours. The marriage between Jesus and the church doesn't get its substance from the faithfulness of those who make up God's people, but from the faithfulness of their God. The prophet Hosea affirms this with great affection:

> *"And in that day, declares the LORD, you will call me 'My Husband,' . . . And I will betroth you to me forever. I will betroth you to me in righteousness and in justice, in steadfast love and in mercy. I will betroth you to me in faithfulness. And you shall know the LORD." (Hosea 2:16, 19–20)*

My dad wasn't alone in seeing his bride with great affection. Christ, who has for himself the church as his bride, holds her as his beloved. He does not just serve her. He is not simply more

fond of her than he is of other people. He has no empty senti-
mentality for her or vain attachment to her. He loves her.

The depiction of God's people as the bride of Christ is one
of the earliest we are given in the Word. It is also the last. In the
book of Revelation, as God pulls back the curtains of eternity to
give us a glimpse of what is to come, he tells us the role we will
play:

> Let us rejoice and be glad
>   and give him glory!
> For the wedding of the Lamb has come,
>   **and his bride has made herself ready**.
> (Rev. 19:7 NIV, emphasis mine)

Our final union with Christ will be celebrated with a grand
wedding feast. Not because it's *like* a wedding. But because it is
one.

Because of this grand vision of what the church will one day
be—the bride of Christ in her full glory, presented to the Son in
celebration and full union—God is concerned with the purity of
his church now. Today, in our daily lives and in our local contexts,
God is purifying his people to make her ready for the Groom,
Jesus Christ. This is his end goal: to present the bride to Christ
purified, and without blemish.

> *Christ loved the church and gave himself up for her*
> *to make her holy, cleansing her by the washing with*
> *water through the word, and to present her to him-*
> *self as a radiant church, without stain or wrinkle*
> *or any other blemish, but holy and blameless. (Eph.*
> *5:25b–27 NIV)*

The Church, His Body

If we think the wedding language is too intimate for our polite Sunday company, then we will be shocked by the second theological reality we find in God's Word. More than his bride awaiting union with him, God insists that his people, the church, are his very own body.

> Christ is the head of the church, **his body**, and is himself its Savior. (Eph. 5:23b, emphasis mine)

> Now you are the **body of Christ** and individually members of it. (1 Cor. 12:27, emphasis mine)

The church is the body of Christ because she is the representation of God's presence in this world. As the Spirit of God indwells the people of God, he unites them to the Son and to each other. The incarnate Christ was the physical presence of God in this world when he walked this earth; now, the church, by the indwelling of his Spirit, is the physical dwelling place of God, the manifestation of his presence in this world.

To get a picture of what it means to be the body, we need look no further than our own skin. Even though we live in a disembodied culture in the West—where online communities are prized, where we tuck (or snip) away any uncomfortable bits of flesh, in which we filter out our physical deficiencies before displaying our image to the world—we know what it means to be a body. Everything we do, and everything we are, resides within our flesh and bones. We have no experience of life apart from the body; we know no service or spirituality apart from the frame we have been given.

This is why to care for our neighbors requires that we do something in our bodies—whether we make a meal, rake their yard, or sit with them, we do it in our bodies. It's our bodies that enable our ministry and give substance to our claims of love.

And God does the same thing for the world he loves. He serves communities, calls the lost, reassures the weak, strengthens the fearful, and feeds the hungry all through his body. The church is not God's make-shift plan to love the world. As David Platt once put it, "The church is God's plan A. There is no plan B."[3]

God calls his church to live into her identity as his body as she faithfully represents his presence in the world through service, worship, witness, and more. And he has equipped us for this work by giving us each unique roles and gifts for service inside and outside of the church:

> *For as in one body we have many members, and the members do not all have the same function, so we, though many, are one body in Christ, and individually members one of another. Having gifts that differ according to the grace given to us, let us use them: if prophecy, in proportion to our faith; if service, in our serving; the one who teaches, in his teaching; the one who exhorts, in his exhortation; the one who contributes, in generosity; the one who leads, with zeal; the one who does acts of mercy, with cheerfulness. (Rom. 12:4–9)*

In the church, we are joined inextricably to other believers and become "members of one another." And yet God has called and gifted us as individuals such that we have something unique to offer to the body of Christ.

When I was in high school, I was on the diving team. I worked really hard for my first three years on the team, and by my senior year, I finally made it to state. I made the hours-long drive to the meet with my team, stretched for warm-ups, and located my family in the bleachers. Then, during one of my

---

[3] David Platt, *Radical: Taking Back Your Faith from the American Dream* (Colorado Springs: Multnomah Books, 2010), 156.

warm-up dives, I hit my feet on the board and broke one of my toes (the one who ate roast beef).

Though it didn't seem like a huge deal at the time—I mean, I still had nine other good toes!—it was the end of my diving career. I couldn't bear weight properly on that foot, and while I could manage an approach and could even wince my way through a jump, my balance was off. All because that one, teeny-tiny toe bone was broken.

This is God's design and good desire for the church. Just like our physical bodies are thrown out of balance when one part is injured or absent, God has seen it fit to design his people in such a way that they need each other. They are not just unified into a homogeneous blob with a singular identity; no, he calls individuals to be an essential part of something bigger than themselves. And, giving them spiritual gifts, he makes them crucial to the health of the whole.

Global and Local

When we talk about the church, we are not just talking about our little local congregation—but we are also not *not* talking about that. The body of Christ is a global and historic reality that is comprised of local bodies that live out these theological realities in their own context. And we all need each other.

The body of Christ around the world and throughout history is made up of different cultures, nations, and contexts. Living out the essentials of the Christian faith have looked different in different eras of church history and across different languages and cultures. We do well when we learn from the church in the past; we can celebrate her resilience, learn from her mistakes, and stand on her shoulders as we benefit from the theological and biblical resources she has left us as our inheritance. We can remember the early church's fire, the passion for purity of those at the theological counsels, the compassion of the monastic movement, the righteous anger of the reformers, and the zeal of the evangelists.

Similarly, the body of Christ today is also made up of local congregations around our communities, nation, and world. We, too, need each other. We have so much to learn from Christian traditions not our own, whether they be the vibrant life in the Spirit moving across Latin America today, the evangelistic fervency of Asian believers, the deep roots of historic faith in Africa, or the love for sound doctrine in the little Baptist church down the street.

Enacting the Salvation Story

God's global body is comprised of local bodies of Christ who are worshiping him and serving his people. And the church—both global and local—is the primary place where we live out the realities of our faith. God has seen fit that the church stand apart from non-profits and Christian associations as something distinct: she has a unique commission and a unique calling. And we see this embodied in the two practices God has commanded upon her as his body: baptism and the Lord's Supper.

Have you ever wondered what makes your local church any different than the campus ministry in town? Have you questioned if you can go to a neighborhood Christian book club and count it as Sunday church? What makes the local church unique from missions organizations and relief groups? After all, isn't the church commanded to evangelize students, study the Word, and aid the poor?

One major distinguishing feature is this: none other than the local church has been commanded to welcome people into the covenant family of God through baptism and to rehearse God's ongoing faithfulness to that covenant through the Lord's Supper. In baptism, people on the outside are brought into the family of God, made members of the body, and are included in the bride of Christ. This is our commission: "Go and make disciples of all nations, baptizing them in the name of the Father and of the Son and of the Holy Spirit" (Matt. 28:19 NIV). In the Lord's Supper, we rehearse the reality of our union with Christ; we remember that by faith in his broken body and shed blood, his death, and his resurrection, we are made one with him in salvation, and we anticipate the day when we will fully and finally be united to him. This is our calling: "This cup is the new covenant in my blood. Do this, as often as you drink it, in remembrance of me" (1 Cor. 11:25).

In commissioning us to baptize and commanding us to set the table with communion, Jesus had one group in mind: his church. These commands were not directed to a random gathering of Christians at a coffee shop or even to a Christian company. No, these practices (some call them *ordinances*, others call them *sacraments*) were directed to God's people as his church, and it is a holy charge she alone holds. And as local churches embrace this commission and calling, we have the distinct privilege of rehearsing the gospel story again and again. We view God's kingdom expansion from front row seats every time someone is baptized; we enact the message of hope found in the resurrected body of Christ each time we approach the table. The joy that this commission and calling is for the church—and, for no other—is unequaled.

The Flock of God

The last biblical image we will consider is the church as the flock of God. Throughout the Scriptures, God calls his people his sheep and reminds us that he is the good Shepherd. Where the images of a bride and body reveal the intimacy God has with his people, no image better reveals God's compassionate heart for his people.

> *He will feed his flock like a shepherd,*
>   *He will carry the lambs in his arms,*
> *holding them close to his heart.*
>   *He will gently lead the mother sheep with their*
>   *young. (Isa. 40:11 NLT)*

David, Israel's hero king and victorious warrior, knew the tenderness of God through this imagery. This is why he reflects on the goodness and mercy of God by saying, "The LORD is my shepherd; I shall not want" (Ps. 23:1).

Sheep are wayward and wandering—as is God's flock. They require not a stiffer arm or a tighter leash, but a tender Shepherd to guide and guard them. After decades of walking with God and an acute experience of shepherding his own literal flock, David finds himself pleading with the Lord to save Israel from her sin and her enemies. He begs the Lord to hear their cries for help, to extend them unearned mercy, and to keep them from being dragged away by the wicked. He asks God to be their shield, strength, and help. And then he concludes with this simple phrase: "Be their shepherd and carry them forever" (Ps. 28:9).

God's people—you and me and every individual united to Christ in faith—are members of God's flock, his church. We are vulnerable and foolish, and he guards us. We are wayward and wandering, and he guides us. We are limping and weak, and he carries us.

The Angry Shepherd

At the beginning of this chapter, I invited us to catch a glimpse of what the church *can* be—to lay aside any painful experiences we have had in local church contexts, and to try to capture God's vision for his people. But that does not mean we pretend that sin and brokenness in the church do not exist. God is indifferent to the wounds caused by his people. Instead, we find God's compassion and righteous anger rising and falling together. Just like a father is most angered when his daughter is wrongfully hurt, so God, because he loves his church the deepest, is most righteously outraged when she is intentionally wounded.

God has called fallen humans to lead his church. One of the many names given to them in the Word is under-shepherds; they are to care for God's sheep with the same compassion, care, tenderness, and concern as the great Shepherd does—and they are accountable to him in doing so (Heb. 13:7; 1 Pet. 5:1–4).

When God's people were being mistreated by under-shepherds in the Old Testament, we see the heart of God come to the rescue of his people and his wrath bring judgment on those who neglected their call to mirror his character as they lead God's people.

> *"This is what the Sovereign LORD says: Woe to you shepherds of Israel who only take care of yourselves! Should not shepherds take care of the flock? You eat the curds, clothe yourselves with the wool and slaughter the choice animals, but you do not take care of the flock. You have not strengthened the weak or healed the sick or bound up the injured. You have not brought back the strays or searched for the lost. You have ruled them harshly and brutally. So they were scattered because there was no shepherd, and when they were scattered they became food for all the wild animals. My sheep wandered over all the mountains and on every high hill. They were scattered over the whole earth, and no one searched or looked for them.*
>
> *. . . therefore, you shepherds, hear the word of the LORD: This is what the Sovereign LORD says: I am against the shepherds and will hold them accountable for my flock." (Ezek. 34:2–6, 9–10 NIV)*

Abuse, neglect, mistreatment, and sin in the church does not go unnoticed by the good Shepherd. He sees. He keeps count. He saves. He heals.

This is particularly poignant for me—I am both someone who has experienced acute church hurt, and I am urged to trust God to hold those who have mistreated me to account (which means I can and must release any bitterness, resentment, or desire to prove myself over to God). And, I am also called to minister in my local church—a ministry of caring for and guiding his people—and I am urged to constantly humble myself before God, asking for his grace to steward this call well, his guidance to keep me from failing. No matter where we find ourselves—broken and bitter or fearful of failing—the heart of the Good Shepherd moves us to humility and surrender.

The Upside-Down Way of the Kingdom

God's vision for his people is grand, but it is also subversive. God has called his people into a radical new identity, and commissioned them into a new way of living. This new way is the way of his kingdom, and we'll find time and time again that it is upside-down from the way the world around us operates.

God has called his church to live out Scripture's "one anothers," which means that our individual lives will look different from our neighbors, and our corporate lives together will create a distinct economy that flies in the face of human wisdom. Where the world tells us to seek honor and esteem, Christ calls his church to honor others above themselves (Rom. 12:10). Where the world insists that we reject those who look, think, or value things differently than we do, Christ calls his church to be like-minded toward one another (Rom. 15:5), accept one another (Rom. 15:7), and be devoted to one another (Rom. 12:10). The world will tell us to look out for ourselves or no one else will; but Jesus tells his church to care for one another (1 Cor. 12:25), be kind and compassionate to one another (Eph. 4:32), bear with one another (Col. 3:13), comfort and encourage one another (1 Thess. 4:18; 5:11).

In the world greed is the rule, but in the church we show each other hospitality (1 Pet. 4:9) and clothe ourselves in humility toward one another (1 Pet. 5:5). The world tells us to put our best face forward and to hold a grudge as leverage when needed; but the church is the place we are to confess our faults to one another (James 5:16) and forgive one another (Eph. 4:32).

As we, God's church, embrace our calling to live called-out lives as the body of believers, our personal lives will look different and our corporate lives together will be distinct as they are marked with the humility, kindness, and compassion of love. And all of this is not just for the sake of being abnormal; it's for the salvation of the world.

> *"By this all people will know that you are my disciples, if you have love for one another." (John 13:35)*

Worshiping the God of the Church

God has a glorious vision of and plan for his church—and you are a part of that. If you are in Christ, you are not only a new creation personally, but you are a brick in the building, a member of the family, a priest in the priesthood, and a sheep in his flock. You are an essential part of God's church, and he invites you to respond to his call in worship.

There are several ways we respond to ecclesiology (theology of the church) in worship, but the first seems so obvious it could go without saying. Unfortunately, for many of us, it does not. If you are a member of the global church—meaning, if you have been personally united to Christ—God desires for you to be a member of a local body where he is worshiped, his Word is opened and honored, and his people serve one another with joy.

The author of Hebrews may have been addressing a culture similar to our own—one in which people wonder what the value of the local church really is, and hoping we can get by with a podcast on the couch on Sunday mornings. But God encourages us with this admonition:

> *And let us consider how to stir up one another to love and good works, **not neglecting to meet together**, as*

is the habit of some, but encouraging one another,
and all the more as you see the Day drawing near.
(Heb. 10:24–25, emphasis mine)

God delights in the corporate praises of his people. In a way that we cannot honor him on our own in our daily quiet times, God is honored as his people gather to sing, read, worship, encourage, fellowship, and praise him together. God's vision of the church extends to you and me a privilege we do not deserve: to give him proper glory in the gathering of his people. That we as sin-riddled people can come into his presence and publicly profess his worth, thereby giving him glory, is perhaps the chief honor of our lifetime.

Serve and Be Filled Up

I came to Grace Church after a particularly hard season of church life. I was dry and weary. Church hurt had left me building walls higher than ever before, and so my heart scoffed when I saw the words on my new pastor's calendar:

"He who refreshes others will himself be refreshed."
(Prov. 11:25)

I didn't believe it. Having nothing left to give, I resolved right there that I would resist serving in this new local church because I felt I didn't have anything left to give. It was the church's turn, in my estimation, to fill *me* up.

But this resolve found me frustrated. No matter what I asked for or demanded of the local church, it didn't satisfy. I said I wouldn't serve until I had counseling, or until I had settled in our new home, or until I made deep connections. And even though believers were reaching out to invite me into those very things I said I wanted, I found the inverse in experience: I was still empty, still dry, still defensive.

It was in this season that the pastor and his wife gently issued me a challenge: serve anyway. Encouraging me to take God at his word and trust the wisdom of this proverb, they encouraged me to serve even when I felt weak and weary, and to trust that God would fill me up as his Word promises.

In the weeks that followed, I found myself reluctantly joining a small group, volunteering to teach a class, and saying yes when invited to serve on Sundays. At first, each yes felt like a burden. I wanted my time to myself in my home on my couch (of course, my audible rationale was much more sophisticated, but it basically boiled down to more time for Netflix).

But those yeses have been some of the best commitments I ever made. The small group Austin and I led landed us some of the best friends we will know in this lifetime, a couple who later said yes to helping us plant a church in a town thirty miles away. Teaching that class led me to teaching a national workshop, an honor that, upon reflection, pales in comparison to the joy of seeing every-day Christians in my local church grasp and savor God's Word in a new way. Each time I obediently served the body as God led, I relinquished a little bit more of my tight fist of control and deliberate sourness; and, I miraculously found, that open hand was filled by God with grace upon grace and more joy than my heart could hold.

Serving at Grace Church on Sundays is now a relished memory—a time when there was a need, I could fill it, and people were blessed as a result. And, just as God promised, I was as well.

We worship God as we choose to live according to his economy, not the world's (and not our own). It is an act of faith and trust to believe that God's ways are better—that generosity in the church will not lead to our personal lack, but to the benefit of all (Luke 6:38); that our service will not dry us up, but will counterintuitively refresh us (Prov. 11:25).

God has gifted you with unique spiritual gifts—gifts that are not meant for you alone, but for the benefit of the body. This means that, by God's design, the gift is in the service. The only way to receive these gifts is to discover them and grow in using them with wisdom and generosity as you serve his church.

The Choir of the Faithful

Have you ever noticed that one of the only places we sing corporately is in the church? You might sing along to the radio in the car, or hum along with your headphones, but I'd bet the only place you lift your voice in unison with other people is within the doors of a local church.

Singing is powerful by design. The psalmist tells us that the praises of God's people become his home—God inhabits his people's worship (Ps. 22:3). But church worship is more than the tunes and hymns. When God's people sing together, they proclaim in unison what they believe about who God is, what he has done, and what he will yet do.

Singing with other believers is like joining in a local creed. As our voices melt together into a single melody, we become a vibrant, unified proclamation of the truths of the gospel. On any given Sunday, our united confession likely includes:

> In Christ alone, my hope is found. He is my light, my strength, my song.[4]

> Our sins they are many, his mercy is more.[5]

> How deep the Father's love for us, how vast beyond all measure.[6]

Many of us will not be able to shake the ordinary nature of this habit, especially if we grew up in the local church. But if we were able to gain proper perspective, we would see what a witness

---

[4] "In Christ Alone (My Hope Is Found)" written by Stuart Townend and Keith Getty.

[5] "His Mercy Is More" written by Matt Boswell and Matt Papa.

[6] "How Deep the Father's Love for Us" written by Stuart Townend.

every experience of corporate worship is. While the world disagrees and when the Enemy tries to silence, the church continues proclaiming in unison her Savior's victory over sin and death. When the lost need hope or the discouraged Christian needs bolstered, the church continues singing of Christ's deep love for her. Like a mantra that keeps on marching, the sung testimony of the church is unending, ongoing, and continuous. Week after week after week, voices lift above the bustle and proclaim eternal truth about salvation, the gospel, the church and her God.

It should amaze us that the unified voice that resiliently proclaims our great God is comprised of voices of the ordinary faithful. Individuals like you and like me are a part of lifting the melody into the air, letting our voice mingle with others' in a song of redemption and profession of God's goodness. As each of our voices—in tune or out—join together, we have the joy of being a part of the song of God's goodness.

And I will promise you this: few things will reinforce your faith like when you look around you during worship and see the young mother you know is battling postpartum depression who presses the words from her lips: "In Christ alone, my hope is found. He is my light, my strength, my song."

Or, when you see the local business leader who publicly fell into sin tearfully sing the song of repentance mingled with hope: "Our sins they are many, his mercy is more."

Or, when you see the young couple who has been job hunting for months, who you know feels financially desperate and discouraged: "How deep the Father's love for us, how vast beyond all measure."

When we know the people behind the voices, the witness takes full form: the local church really is an outpost of the kingdom of God, upside-down from the ways of this world, and a place of resilient faith. Though she be deeply flawed, the church is God's beloved, his redeemed, his body, his song of witness calling out to a dying world.

Do you want to know what's sweet? God has made your voice essential to that melody. He has called you to be an integral member of his body, a joyful participant in the life of his flock, and an ever-growing, ever-purified member of his bride. And he invites you to lift up your head, fix your eyes on him, and join in that song.

Eschatology: Worshiping
the Coming King

If Jesus is still dead, then our faith is fake, our guilt
is real, and our hope is naïve optimism. . . .
But Jesus is not dead. . . . The kingdom is
advancing because the king is alive.[1]

Jeremy Treat

I sat in the back seat of my sister's car in silence. While my siblings laughed at inside jokes from Thanksgivings past, I had a pit in my stomach and a lump in my throat preventing me from joining in.

We were all home from college for the short Thanksgiving break, and were heading back to our parents' house after lunch together at a favorite hometown diner. While at lunch, I had caught a snippet of the news on a TV that hung against the back wall of the diner, and the reporter was foreboding. A war raging somewhere just beyond our borders, threats of violence creeping closer to home, food shortages of which I was blissfully unaware.

---

[1] Jeremy R. Treat, *Seek First: How the Kingdom of God Changes Everything* (Grand Rapids: Zondervan, 2019), 57–58.

The world seemed to be growing darker by the minute. Adding to my anxiety was my current class list in Bible school, which included a class that covered the end times. I had recently (and reluctantly) read the book of Revelation, and, combining what I was learning about the end times with this news report, I was terrified that it was all coming to an end.

You might chuckle at my doomsday outlook (and I can join you from where I sit now), but in that moment, the impending fate of the world felt very real to me. As a student of the Bible, I took the book of Revelation seriously. I believed (and still do) that we can take the Scriptures to the bank; that the Word is worth its salt. What the book of Revelation was telling me was going to happen was really, actually going to happen. And it shook me to my core.

Fearing the End Times

Maybe you've felt this fear before. The book of Revelation is one that you're not inclined to read because, if we're honest, it's confusing and a bit scary. Or maybe you wondered about the end times and decided to read the book of Revelation, but were left with more questions than answers. Add to Revelation's complicated structure the endless movies and books that depict the end of the world in the grimmest terms and darkest details, this isn't a conversation that many of us want to have. We may want clarity, but the journey there feels uncertain and unsettling, and so we'd just rather stick with reading the book of James (again).

For many of us, these waters can feel so murky that we forget that the title of this book underscores its purpose: Revelation is all about the great reveal. When we zoom out from the details of the book of prophecy and remember its overall intent, we remember that Revelation is all about *revelation*; its purpose is divine divulgence and heavenly exposure. What John, the author of the book of Revelation, was given was a vision of what lies beyond the heavenly veil: both the economy of heaven and the events that will unfold as that economy collides with earth. What John recorded for us, by the power of the Holy Spirit, is the great unveiling, the pulling back of the curtain that stands between us and eternity. That's what the book of Revelation is all about.

Here, I want to remind us of something foundational. You are not reading this chapter to obtain a theology of the end times (formally called *eschatology*). You are not here in order to gain a view of what is to come in the final days of this world. You already have one. What you believe is behind that curtain *is* your theology of final things. Whether you believe the curtain will be drawn to reveal the great doomsday of all mankind or an endless buffet of sweets and countless rounds of golf for generically good people—*that* is your theology of final things.

Reading Revelation

One of the things I least wanted to do in my seminary career is the very thing I am most grateful to have completed during that season of education. All students in the Masters of Divinity program had to take Greek and Hebrew, the two primary languages the Bible was originally written in. After we had completed the basic grammar classes in both languages, we could choose to study two books of the Bible written in that language. I eagerly took Genesis and Job in Hebrew, and completed the Gospel of Mark in Greek. With one more Greek class to choose, I looked at that semester's offerings: Matthew or Revelation. The choice would be easy. There was nothing in me that wanted to study Revelation for an entire semester (plus Matthew seemed like an easy A, having already completed another gospel book).

But because I lived with a fear of the end times—albeit residual and pushed into the back of my mind and theology—my husband encouraged me to take Revelation. The surge of anxiety that swelled within me at his suggestion was all the convincing I needed. I knew I needed to take a close look at this book that stirred such fright and avoidance in me. And so, hemming and hawing, I enrolled.

What I learned in that class lead me to make what might be one of the most surprising statements I have ever heard come from my own lips: Revelation now ranks among my favorite books of the Bible. For all its exegetical complexities, Revelation holds out for believers an abundant hope for life beyond this world, and gives us a glorious picture of the God of all things.

Maintaining the Mystery

Our culture doesn't like unsolved mysteries. Look no further than the litany of crime shows that follow a predictable formula. We want to have all the answers laid out soothingly before us. We want to see how the story will come together. And, more than anything, we love being able to figure it out before the big reveal at the end.

This is a good impulse in our world. It is good to want to uncover the key clues or answer the lingering question of "who done it?" But this impulse is only good because we are not; because we live in a fallen world, "mystery" is often concealing something that is malicious, dark, and broken that needs to be exposed. Where we find mystery, it is our human impulse to try to find answers—to chart out the time line, to read between the lines, to map and graph and explain away the tension that mysteries brew within us.

But God is not like us. Within the prophetic passages on the life to come—whether in Christ's final words during passion week, Daniel's prophecy about the final coming of the King, or Revelation's words on God's new creation—God has chosen to maintain an element of mystery. While he has given us everything we need to know to have hope for the future and to live today with conviction, he has not given us a detailed time line or a newspaper in advance. Instead, he has given us sure promises tinged with a bit of holy mystery.

And unlike our world in which mysteries often conceal something that is worse than we can imagine, in God's economy, the mystery conceals something that is *better* than we can imagine. God has written our future hope enshrouded in divine concealment that leaves us with a bit of tension in our stomachs and uncertainty about the details—and this is our good. The reality of the hope to come is better than our fallen human minds and hearts could ever, ever contain.

Say What We Can, Not More Than We Can

It's worth noting something important here. There's a *reason* we pull back from these passages of Scripture and from this theological conversation—and it's because it's complicated. We can't pretend that the conversation on the end times is clear or cut-and-dried. That would be both foolish and dishonest.

These conversations concerning the life to come are complex, to be sure. And so it is essential that we navigate them with care. Their complexity shouldn't stop us from diving headlong into the study of the book, but they should also give us meekness enough to recognize our human limitations. It's a work of diligence to study the Scriptures so that we can agree with them on what they say about the end times; it's a work of humility to ensure that we don't say *more* than the Scriptures say about the end times.

And so in this chapter my aim is to say with confidence what we can say—to agree with God's Word in what it clearly holds out for as our hope for an eternal future. But we will also stop short of answering all the questions we may have about the end times. The task before us is to, with one hand, grasp with confidence an orthodox theology of the end times, and with the other, hold out a palm of creaturely humility that is decidedly open to divine mystery.

Narrowing the Conversation: Final Things

The conversation on end times theology is wide and wondering. Flip open any given written work on the topic and the contents are as different as the author's personalities and perspectives. This theological conversation can encapsulate a large spectrum as it seeks to make sense of physical death and resurrection, the Revelation vision of the new creation and New Jerusalem, and the mercy and judgement of God. Some consider questions surrounding where are deceased believers now (heaven? paradise?) and the spiritual experience between a person's death and the resurrection of her body, while others focus on the events that will take place as a sign that Christ's return is near (and the order in which these landmark events will unfold). Still others seek to underline the importance and task of faithfully reading the book of Revelation and other apocalyptic literature.

This conversation has a grand scope and, for our purposes, I want to narrow our focus and consider a theology of *final things*—or the events that God has promised through the witness of his Word will take place at the culmination of the story of redemption. I want to invite us to consider what, at the end of all things, God has promised will be—namely the new heavens and new earth pictured in the book of Revelation—and what it means for our lives today.

This is not to say that the other topics are less important or essential in the life of Christian theology. But I do choose this focus for this reason: what we believe about our final destination as believers will shape how we view most other related questions on the topic of end times theology. The promise that Scripture holds out to us of a future life with Christ for all of eternity—and how we conceive of that promise's fulfillment—will give shape to what we believe happens in physical death, the centrality (or decentralization) of the resurrection of the body, and how we live in light of this very real hope in our present life.

Because of this, our task in this chapter is not to understand every theological perspective that exists on the topic, but to lift our chins upward. To pick our heads up above the details and minutia of end times theological "camps" and to ask a bigger question—where is this Christian life heading, anyway?

Revelation 21

God has been telling us about this destination throughout his Word. We find whispers of the promise of what is to come as early as Genesis 3 when God assures humanity that one day the serpent's head will be crushed for good. Throughout the Old Testament, God speaks through prophets like Daniel and Ezekiel to give his people a picture of what will happen in their day and in the ultimate age to come. But in no place is a theology of final things prized more heavily than in Revelation 21. John, in a vision of the final things of this world, is given a glimpse of the world as God sees it—the garden serpent has become a dragon that wages war on God's people; the empire that oppresses and seduces God's chosen, from heaven's perspective, is a harlot. Through a series of events and judgments, God drops the eternal gavel of justice as he proclaims that the war is over, his people are saved, and his kingdom has come in full.

And then, in verses 2–5, John writes this:

> *And I saw the holy city, new Jerusalem, coming down out of heaven from God, prepared as a bride adorned for her husband. And I heard a loud voice from the throne saying, "Behold, the dwelling place of God is with man. He will dwell with them, and they will be his people, and God himself will be with them as their God. He will wipe away every tear from their eyes, and death shall be no more, neither shall there be mourning, nor crying, nor pain any-more, for the former things have passed away." And*

he who was seated on the throne said, "Behold, I am
making all things new." Also he said, "Write this
down, for these words are trustworthy and true."

The events outlined in these short, content-packed verses
are the destination of the Christian life, the X on our theological
map. Line-by-line, John's prophecy showcases a countercultural
future reality for Christians and holds out a profound hope for
us as we consider our own theology of what is to come. It may
require us to abandon some of our own cultural truisms about the
end times, but as we unpack what John means in these verses, we
will see that the exchange is only ever in our favor.

New Jerusalem

"And I saw the holy city, new Jerusalem, coming
down out of heaven from God, prepared as a bride
adorned for her husband." (Rev. 21:2)

The story that began in a paradise garden culminates in a
holy city, the New Jerusalem. God, in his divine plan of redemption, has built for his people a redeemed metropolis where they
will dwell, unhindered and unobstructed, with him.

This heavenly city is the fulfillment of God's plan of redemption from the very beginning. When God commissions his people at the dawn of time, he gives them a charge—a task that
identifies the very purpose for which he made them. Having just
created man and woman, God proclaims that they, his creation,
are very good, and he tells them to be fruitful and multiply; they
are to have dominion and fill the earth.

"He is," pastor-theologian Tim Keller says, "directing them
to build a God-honoring civilization. They are to bring forth

the riches that God put into creation by developing science, art, architecture, human society."[2]

In short, mankind was originally tasked with partnering with God in creating a society that mines the riches of God's creation—harnessing the raw materials of God's good earth, and cultivating them until they reached their fullest potential, whether that be in food or beauty or innovation. And, they were to order those God-designed elements in such a way that the glory of God's presence was magnified. In other words, the abundance of mankind that has filled the earth can enjoy the abundance of God's presence in a city that glorifies and enjoys its Maker.

And we all know what happened. Sin wrecked everything.

The sin that entered the economy of the garden wove its way through the very foundations of God's perfect world, leaving nothing unaffected. Now man's chief charge of being fruitful and multiplying was wracked with pain in childbearing and thorns that choked the fruit of the earth; the human's holy dominion was now bent and twisted with pride and disordered with rebellion. The city of God was exchanged in the fall for a city of men—the city we have been living in ever since.

The hope of the Christian life is that God is going to undo all the wreckage of the fall and establish his holy city, the New Jerusalem. "This city is the Garden of Eden, remade. The City is the fulfillment of the purposes of the Eden of God."[3] God is not trashing his original plan and making something entirely new; instead, he is bringing to ultimate fulfillment his vision for a holy economy, a God-saturated civilization where he dwells with his creation, unhindered and unimpeded.

---

[2] Timothy Keller, "A Theology of Cities," Cru.org, www.cru.org/us/en /train-and-grow/leadership-training/sending-your-team/a-theology-of -cities.html. Accessed November 9, 2020.

[3] Ibid.

And we can't help but notice that mankind is not ascending to God for this New Jerusalem; it is coming down from God. God's world, as it were, is colliding with our world and having the restorative dominion that we failed to have. God's economy of heaven—his ways of justice and redemption and peace and faithfulness and perfect love—comes crashing into our broken, sin-ravaged world. Revelation gives us no indication that mankind is incrementally improving himself as he builds God's city through self-betterment. No, God is doing what only God can do: he is making our world his world in the fullness of redemption.

This means two very poignant things for us. First, this verse in Revelation reveals itself to be the fulfillment of the prayer Jesus taught his disciples to pray. In the Lord's prayer, Jesus taught the twelve (and us) to pray for God's will to be done "on earth as it is in heaven." Revelation gives us confidence that God's answer to that prayer is an earth-shattering (or more appropriately, earth-*renewing*) and eternally-resounding *"Yes."* One day, the will of God will be perfectly done on earth when he brings his holy city to earth at the end of all time.

Secondly, this verse puts to an end any notions we have about a cloudy, harp-playing heavenly existence. It leaves us with no inclinations that we will be remade as chubby little cherubs with wings and halos (how disappointing that would be in comparison!). Just as John recognized the descent of God's world as the New Jerusalem, we can have confidence that God's world will be God's good Edenic intentions in its full and final form—a heavenly city that resembles what we know and love about God's good creation now, but one that is untainted by sin and unencumbered by the fall.

It's important that we say with humility that we do not know the minutia of what this city will be like. We don't want to extrapolate these verses out farther than they were intended. But I do believe these verses give us confidence to say a few things about the destination of the Christian life. The very fact that God's original intention for mankind was the holy work of caring for creation and the future reality of an eternal city remind us that work is not a result of the fall, but a reality that flows from the heart of God. In the garden as well as in the new creation, mankind will partner with God in creating, working, ordering, and cultivating the world in accordance with God's character. Mankind will flourish through the very things God has created for our enjoyment and his glory—we can estimate that cooking and art and architecture and poetry and agriculture and science will all find their final and restored form and we delight in the presence of God in the fullness of his redemption city.

At the end of all things, God is going to usher his economy into the world. This isn't a rewind to the garden, but a thrusting forward of God's vision for the world. This isn't a reset on creation, but a culmination of everything that lies in the heart of God. This is not Eden—it's even better.

God's Dwelling with Man

The crowning jewel of this new world, however, is not the things man does in the redeemed world—it is the One at the center of it all.

> *And I heard a loud voice from the throne saying,*
> *"Behold, the dwelling place of God is with man. He*
> *will dwell with them, and they will be his people,*
> *and God himself will be with them as their God."*
> *(Rev. 21:3)*

What makes this city the holy place that it is, is the Holy One. God has come to dwell with man in the fullness of his glory.

To be with his creation has been in God's heart from the beginning, which is why the story of redemption throughout the entire Bible is one of God's ongoing and persistent pursuit of his people. Though they were cast from his presence at the Fall, God moved toward them. He came to them in veiled ways that they could see and understand—in burning bushes and thunder clouds and still, small voices. He established a place where they could meet—the tabernacle—where he would guide them and give them a means by which their sins could be forgiven. God took up residence among them in the temple, dwelling among his people with a firm foundation of fixed centrality and communal glory. Then God came right into the heart of his broken creation—moving so close to his people that he became flesh—born a feeble infant in a manger in order to buy back his world from the Fall. And, ultimately, God came even closer—going from "God *with* us" in the person of Christ to "God *in* us" through the person of the Holy Spirit.

God has been moving toward his people chapter-by-chapter in the grand narrative of his Word. And, in the end, God will come and dwell with his people. Unhindered, unencumbered, unchained by sin and the Fall, God will dwell with those who are his. They will finally be his people forever; they will have him as their God eternally. The proximity of presence that has always been God's desire and his people's greatest good will become ultimate and final reality.

This is the culmination of our union with Christ. Those who are in Christ in this world will be found in Christ in his holy city. This is why it is called the "consummation" of all things: because the union we have with Christ in salvation now will take its fullest form as we savor our richest intimacy and inseparable oneness with him. We will be with Christ and in Christ forever as we worship the risen Savior of our union face-to-face.

Evil Vanquished

> *"He will wipe away every tear from their eyes, and death shall be no more, neither shall there be mourning, nor crying, nor pain anymore, for the former things have passed away." (Rev. 21:4)*

Our present reality in this world is this: everyone and everything dies. God warned us in the garden that sin would lead to death—both physical and spiritual death—and his warning has proved true. There is nothing in this world that has in itself eternal life; plants and animals, friends and loved ones die. Death is inevitable. It is the way of our broken universe.

But in God's new world, this will no longer be the case. God is rewiring the system, renewing creation in such a way that it operates according to a different set of rules—a former set of rules. Death will no longer be the rule; eternal life will be.

In God's good pleasure, he is making a city in which he will dwell with his people, and there will no longer be the stain of sin that leads to death. In God's holy city, there will be no pain—backs won't ache and hearts won't break. There will be no tears—not for lack of tear ducts, but because there will be no reason for us to shed a tear. There will be no death—life will be the governing principle of the universe. Just as confident as we are in this world that we will one day die, in God's new city we will have the same kind of confidence regarding our life with him. Death will be no more because God and his eternal life has become the way of the universe—forever.

Because of Christ

We've already said that our theology of final things is formed and informed by every other theological topic we have addressed, and I think that is especially the case at this juncture. The reason we can have such confidence that eternal life will be the rule is not only because of this verse in Revelation 21, but also because of what the entire Bible proclaims about Christ.

Jesus defeated death at the empty tomb, and his resurrection victory resounds into eternity. At the resurrection, Jesus pulled at the central thread of our morbid reality, and his victory over death has been unraveling death's clutch on the world ever since. We have confidence that life will be the guiding and guarding principle of this new world because the resurrected Jesus is alive forevermore, and this is *his city*. This is the place he has prepared, and he has poured his character into its very infrastructure. This new city is flooded with his life and light. Death will be no more because the King on the throne is the resurrected Jesus, and death has no place in this kingdom of his love and dominion.

We know that the resurrected Jesus sits on the throne and has dominion even now; and yet sin and its consequences are still present in our world. But at his second coming, when he brings his holy city to collide with our world, his victory over death and sin will take their full form. Or, as theologians like to say, what is his by right will be his by might. The Enemy will be finally defeated, sin and death will be destroyed, and everything that Christ has accomplished will be fully executed in this new world.

All Things New

Into the wonder of John's prophetic vision booms a voice from the throne:

> *And he who was seated on the throne said, "Behold,*
> *I am making all things new." (Rev. 21:5)*

The Creator who spoke the universe into existence speaks once more, and declares that he is doing another creative work. He is going to make the creation that he loves, the creation that he declared very good, the creation that was wrecked by sin, the creation that he moved toward to save, the creation that he is reestablishing as his eternal residence with his people—that creation, he is making new.

The word here for "all" is the Greek word "panta" and it is all-encompassing. There is nothing within God's scope of creative work that will not be renewed in his re-creation work. God isn't running from a burning building and having to grab his favorite things to be rescued while leaving others behind; no, the recreative work of God is as far and wide as creation itself. God is going to make the hummingbirds and golden retrievers new, the cypress trees and sandy beaches new, the galaxies and asteroids new, the human bodies and human hearts new. There is nothing—absolutely nothing—in all of creation that God is not making new in his re-creative act in the new heavens and new earth.

And it's essential that we don't miss something here. Our reminder that grammar is important, we'll notice which of these words play which grammatical role in this tiny little phrase. The word *new* here plays the primary grammatical role in verse, and it describes the final status of the things of creation. It is not just a description that highlight "things." Though this seems technical and perhaps a bit of a flashback to eighth grade English, its ramifications are significant. Grammar is the difference between God declaring that he is making all things *new* and declaring that he is making all new *things*.

It should dumbfound us that it is the former. God is not making all new things; he is not wadding up the heavens and earth as if it were a first draft destined for the trash bin. He is, rather, making all things new. He is doing his transformative, redemptive, re-creative work on the very creation he loves—and nothing is left untouched by his sovereign hand of rejuvenating power.

Resurrection of the Body

Few places is this more keenly on display than in the promise of resurrection life for believers. God is not in the business of replacement; he is in the business of redemption. We need look no further than the resurrected Jesus who rose to life in his crucified body, overcoming the grave and paving the way for our future resurrection. Jesus did not rise from the dead in power in a body no one would recognize as his own, nor did he rise from the dead without the marks of his glorious sacrifice on the cross. The human body wasn't something to be shed as if it tainted his authority and limited his power, but his very body was raised, renewed and transformed in resurrection power.

Christ's resurrection paints a theological outline of what we can expect for our own bodily resurrection when God calls us to himself in the new creation. The future hope of the Christian life isn't a disembodied existence as our souls flit from cloud to cloud. Christ is our forerunner—our very real expectation is that our bodies will be raised like Christ's, renewed like Christ's, and transformed in resurrection power like Christ's! The upward call of heaven is not one that seeks to escape the body, as most religions put forth. Our call is one of renewal and resurrection. And we have this sure hope precisely because Jesus was raised bodily from the dead, ascended into heaven, and now sits at the right hand of God the Father (Rom. 8:34; Eph. 1:20; Col. 3:1; Heb. 1:3, 8:1).

The resurrection of Jesus permanently changed the trajectory of bodies here on earth: we are bound for resurrection! In fact Scripture is clear: *everyone* will be resurrected. Those in Christ will wake to new life with him and those not in Christ will wake to eternal life apart from him (John 5:28–29). Our eternal destinations may be different, but do not be mistaken: all will be raised.

Eternal Death

As we think about the resurrected future of all people, we would be foolish not to consider for a moment one of the sobering implications of the all-encompassing reign of Christ. For those who are in Christ, the new creation is the long-anticipated consummation of that union; but for those who are not in Christ, it is ultimate and final separation from God, or eternal death.

For all the complexities end times theology has, one thing is clear: the new heavens and new earth are filled with God's glory and authority. At that time, the rule of Jesus is final, culminating, and irrevocable. Those who enjoy God's city as citizens are those who have bent their knees to Christ; who have, in faith, agreed with God that he is the only One able to save them from their sins and make them right with the Father; those who carry his indwelling Spirit as a marker and guarantee that they are, indeed, his. And those who have not been reconciled to God through Christ are eternally separated from him in a death that lasts forever.

And this is only proper. From the very first pages of Scripture we are reminded: while God surely desires to make his home with man (Gen. 1–2; John 14:23; Rev. 21:3), his holiness would never allow for him to make his home with sin. Indeed, his holiness repels sin. As the psalmist says about the Lord, "evil may not dwell with you" (Ps. 5:4) This is why humans were banished from the garden of Eden (Gen. 3:23–24) and why God concealed his holy presence from Moses' gaze (Exod. 33:20)—God's holiness is so pure that upon coming in contact with our sin, it would consume us. And so it does for those who have not been cleansed from their sin by the blood of Christ's all-sufficient sacrifice and robed in his righteousness. Instead of dwelling with God forever, those not in Christ will be barred from the holy presence of God and will suffer eternally in hell.

While we may want to shy away from the "messy" doctrine of hell, we cannot have a doctrine of God's holiness any other way. It's God's perfect righteousness that makes hell what it is—a place where his judgment and wrath against sin burn hot and without end. This is, perhaps, why Jesus taught about hell in his earthly ministry more than anyone else in Scripture—because in his great love for us, he desires for us to know the extent of his saving sacrifice for us and to come to him in repentance and be saved.

Though it grieves us deeply that there will be those who are eternally separated from God's presence, we must acknowledge that it is a chosen destination. Those who desire to live apart from God's rule and reign will be given exactly what they desire: to live eternally apart from Christ. Put more starkly, to those who do not say to God, "thy will be done," God will say, "thy will be done," giving them the eternal outcome of their self-chosen flight away from him.[4]

This is why C. S. Lewis describes hell as locked from inside. Having no desire to be in God's presence—no impetus to give him glory and honor, no recognition of his rule and reign, no delight in living in his new city as his people—those separated from God desire to be so. And God will give them over to the eternal outcome of their determined desire to run from him.

And they are not alone. Hell is also the destination of the Enemy of God's people, Satan, and the demons who, with him, rebel against God. The pitchforked comic strips depicting a devil overseeing the torture of those in hell couldn't be further from the truth. Satan himself will be a prisoner of hell; he himself will experience the torment of eternal separation of a good and gracious God. Hell is not a place where evil thrives while heaven is a place where goodness reigns; God is not King of heaven and Satan the ruler of hell. No, hell is a place devoid of God's presence—and all the goodness that accompanies it—and the new creation is a place where every inch is covered in God's unhindered presence.

Even as difficult as it may be for us to understand and theologically digest the reality of hell and those who will experience this separation from God, it is important for us to remember this: a God of justice is the God we want. We want a God of endless glory, love, grace, and mercy; and none of these exist without divine justice and wrath against sin. For rebellion against God to rage on in human hearts in the new heavens and new earth would mar the new creation he is forming; it simply does not

---

[4] Tom Wright, "Ask NT Wright Anything: #39 Will Animals Go to Heaven? . . . And Other Questions on New Creation on Apple Podcasts," *Apple Podcasts*, 30 June 2020, podcasts.apple.com/gb/podcast/39-will-animals-go-to-heaven-other-questions-on-new/id1441656192?i=1000480416847. Accessed November 9, 2020.

belong. In hell, God justly punishes sin and evil, forever removing it from his presence as he reigns over his new creation.

Faithful and True

Also he said, "Write this down, for these words are trustworthy and true." (Rev. 21:5)

Our eschatology (theology of the end times), as we have already said, holds one hand open to the mystery of that which we cannot know or understand. There is much that God has chosen to conceal from us, including the time when he will come and establish the new heavens and new earth. And so we hold these things openhandedly and with the humility that rightly arises from understanding our human limits.

And yet, God has chosen, in his infinite wisdom and sovereignty, to give us a picture of what is to come. To give us instruction and hope, to form our thoughts of him and our anticipation of what lies ahead of us.

So the question for you and I is this: do we believe this? Do we agree with the voice from the throne that these words are faithful and true?

I would like to propose that the answer to this question doesn't come in the form of an internal nodding of our heads, but in how we live our lives in the day-to-day. Whether or not we believe these things to be true will be on display in our daily lives, for, just as with everything else, this theology has far-reaching effects on our daily life of worship.

Rehearsing the Economy of Heaven

The new heavens and new earth give us much to anticipate as we look forward to the day when there will be no pain or tears or death—when God's presence is fully among his people and our union with Christ is thoroughly realized. It is good and right for us to wait for this day with eagerness.

But for those of us who are in Christ, joy is not only ahead; it is now. Today. In this world and in this life.

Right now, God is a God of redemption and renewal. Right now, God loves his creation and is at work in his creation in such a way that we see his grace. Right now, Christ is seated on his throne, his salvation work complete. We are living in what we've come to understand as the "already-not-yet." Even though there is anticipation of the day ahead when sin will be vanquished, today God has given us freedom over sin by the Spirit of God. The economy of God is not only something that lies ahead; it is something we can experience now as we walk in the Spirit and savor our union with the Son.

Today, as we live counterculturally as God's people, we are a part of the breaking in of his kingdom. We, in a sense, are living into the economy of God here and now, even as we anticipate the day when that economy floods the new city. Through our faith over sight, our generosity over greed, our love of neighbor over love of self, our pouring out and being filled up, and our prioritization of the family of faith over worldly affinities, we are choosing to live as citizens of God's kingdom, working according to his will and ways. Our faithful lives of stewardship and joy today are our daily way of saying yes to God and no to the world—until the day heaven comes to earth.

In the great day of Christ's return, I believe we will find two things to be simultaneously true: everything we do here today will have infinitely more meaning in the new heavens and new earth than we ever could have dreamed. The pastries we enjoyed, the music that leads us in worship, the cold cups of water given to someone in need, the heart warmed with gratitude toward God, the prayer for the sick, the offense forgiven, the hot meals put on the dinner table, the seventeenth time of stooping down to answer the question of a little child, the hospitality shown to the lonely—I believe we will look back at all of it completely dumbfounded that God allowed us, in our sinful and broken and in-process state, to participate in the economy of heaven in such a glorious way.

And, simultaneously, I believe we will see God's world with new eyes that are finally able to behold his grandeur. We will stand in awe of a world that we never dreamed could have existed and feel deep in our bones that it is all so good that it must be true. We will worship God with all of our beings and might because we see him in an unrestrained way, and we cannot hold our worship in. We must pour it out. He's just that glorious.

Evangelize

If we were to look at cultural pictures of the apocalypse, we would be filled with doom at the thought of Christ's return. But a look at Revelation unveils a much different picture; the coming of Christ is the coming of our hope and initiation of the new heavens and new earth. It is our joy come to life and our hope fully fashioned.

While we anticipate with joy the destination of our theology, the joy is not for us to keep to ourselves. Out of desire to make Christ known and a passion for others to be united to Christ in salvation as well—out of this outpouring of love for God and neighbor, we share the hope of the gospel with those who are still separated from God.

The burden we feel when we think about our loved ones being separated from God for all of eternity gives us a sober-minded view of God, and it fuels our evangelism. Yet I think there is no better stick to stoke the fires of evangelism in our hearts than the joy of knowing Christ and being found in Him. From a place of purpose rather than begrudging obligation, we can share the call God has sent out into the universe calling unbelievers to find restoration in his Son. With joy, we can join with God in the work of preaching the gospel to a lost and dying world, and then open our hands in surrender to the God who is sovereign over salvation.

Enjoy

I ran my fingers over the thin tulle veil before tucking it behind my wedding dress and zipping the bag shut. Returning it to the wardrobe, I turned around to face a bridal suite full of icons—icons of preparation. The bouquets sat ready in individual vases with boutonnieres resting nearby. Bridesmaid dresses were pressed and waiting, shoes lined up beneath each dress like little soldiers. Downstairs the tables had been decorated with mason jars with tea lights, extra blooms, and old library books (a nod at the texture of our relationship and the hours we spent getting to know each other in the seminary library); table numbers were twisted from faux moss, and name cards sat at the head of each plate in tiny pots holding tiny succulents. Dinner menus were printed, the rings were kept by the best man, and the catering service stood ready with glasses for toasting.

It was the evening before our wedding, and the sentimentalist in me couldn't help but pause and take it all in before heading downstairs to rejoin the wedding party. After what seemed like ages of preparation, everything sat ready and waiting. The past few months had been full of phone calls and planning, addressing envelopes and ordering flowers, finishing seminary finals and finding a new apartment to share with Austin. I had worked constantly toward this moment for months, and now all that was left was to celebrate at the rehearsal dinner with friends and family.

But I had a problem.

As I surveyed what should have been an ideal scene, I couldn't help noticing the nagging pit in my stomach. There was something I hadn't done—right? There was something I should be doing right then—wasn't there? Months of work and effort and budgeting had produced in me this gut-level, knee-jerk reaction:

Shouldn't I be doing something? Shouldn't I be busy? Wasn't there something left for me to worry about or fuss over?

As guests filtered into the venue for the rehearsal dinner, I shared this anxiety with my mom. I figured she would give me some advice for talking to guests or have just one more to-do list item in mind for me. But she left me disappointed in this regard. Instead of telling me which tasks I should take up for the evening, she put her hand gently on my arm and swept her other hand across the room filling with friends.

"Rehearse and enjoy. Everything is ready. The wedding will be here before you know it."

Perhaps you're like me, and you're hoping this chapter concludes with a task list you can check off as you anticipate the coming of the Savior. But I hope to leave you as delightfully disappointed as my mother left me that rehearsal dinner evening. As we await the coming of our King, the Bridegroom of the church and the Savior of our affection, the call on our lives is the same: rehearse and enjoy.

Throughout the book of Revelation, the final consummation of all things is called the wedding feast of the Lamb. And this is not arbitrary or a word picture; it is what is actually happening. The Savior has bought his chosen back, brought her to himself, and will on that day make her his own finally and forever. Listen to how Isaiah prophetically describes what this day will be like:

> On this mountain the Lord Almighty will prepare
>   a feast of rich food for all peoples,
> a banquet of aged wine—
>   the best of meats and the finest of wines.
> On this mountain he will destroy
>   the shroud that enfolds all peoples,
> the sheet that covers all nations;
>   he will swallow up death forever.

> *The Sovereign* LORD *will wipe away the tears*
>   *from all faces;*
> *he will remove his people's disgrace*
>   *from all the earth.*
> *The* LORD *has spoken.*
>
> *In that day they will say,*
> *"Surely this is our God;*
>   *we trusted in him, and he saved us.*
> *This is the* LORD, *we trusted in him;*
>   *let us rejoice and be glad in his salvation."*
> *(Isa. 25:6–9 NIV)*

It will be glorious, and we await this very real future reality
with holy hope in Christ.

But that is not all. Today, we rehearse the realities of the new
heavens and new earth as we live according to God's kingdom
purposes over and against the purposes of the earthly kingdoms
that surround us. If the marriage supper of the Lamb is what
awaits us, then you could say that we are enjoying the rehearsal
dinner of that wedding feast each time we set the table for our
family and community. We practice the ways of the kingdom of
God in our own families, rearranging the economy of our homes
such that they better mirror God's own. The supper will have
room for all, and no one will be shown favoritism; we break in
that same kingdom principle when we show grace to everyone
at our table, regardless of whether or not we find them lovely
or deserving. The supper will have the choicest wine and richest food; and so we set our tables with good things, taking the
time to savor them knowing that God's kingdom is a place called
"rest." The wedding feast will have a central focus on the King
of kings and Lord of lords; and we rehearse that supper reality
when we make Jesus the King of our households, dinner tables,
family, and hearts.

We rehearse . . . and we enjoy. We foster our delight in the God of our salvation, knowing that we are being made more fit for his holy city the more we find pleasure in his presence. We enjoy the good gifts of the earth with faith that God will redeem and restore his creation according to his good delight and purpose. We relish long conversations with friends, full tables and full bellies, knowing that they are a glimpse of what lies ahead.

As we close this weighty topic, I wish to leave you with a weightier hope:

"Rehearse and enjoy. Everything is ready. The wedding will be here before you know it."

Works Cited

St. Athanasius of Alexandra. *St. Athanasius on the Incarnation: The Treatise De Incarnatione Verbi Dei.* Translated and Edited by a Religious of C.S.M.V. London: A. R. Mowbray & Co., 1953.

The Athanasian Creed. http://www.reformedspokane.org/ Doctrine_pages/Christian%20Doctrine%20pages/ Eccumenical%20Creeds/Athanasian%20Creed.html.

Michael F. Bird. *Evangelical Theology, Second Edition: A Biblical and Systematic Introduction.* Grand Rapids: Zondervan, 2020.

Bird, Michael F. *What Christians Ought to Believe: An Introduction to Christian Doctrine through the Apostles' Creed.* Grand Rapids: Zondervan, 2016.

Butterfield, Rosaria. *The Secret Thoughts of an Unlikely Convert: An English Professor's Journey into Christian Faith.* Pittsburgh: Crown & Covenant Publications, 2014.

Calvin, John, and Joseph Haroutunian, ed. "Preface to Olivétan's New Testament." *Calvin: Commentaries.* Philadelphia: Westminster Press, 1958.

Calvin, John, et al. *Institutes of the Christian Religion.* Louisville, KY: Westminster John Knox Press, 2011.

Clark, John C., and Marcus Peter Johnson. *The Incarnation of God: The Mystery of the Gospel as the Foundation of Evangelical Theology*. Wheaton, IL: Crossway, 2015.

Edwards, Jonathan. *The Works of Jonathan Edwards. Vol. 23 The "Miscellanies."* New Haven: Yale University Press, 2004.

Fee, Gordon D. *Paul, the Spirit, and the People of God*. Grand Rapids: Baker Academic, 2011.

Frame, John M. "The Omnipotence, Omniscience, and Omnipresence of God." *The Gospel Coalition*, www.the gospelcoalition.org/essay/omnipotence-omniscience -omnipresence-god/.

Horton, Michael. *Pilgrim Theology: Core Doctrines for Christian Disciples*. Grand Rapids: Zondervan, 2011.

Johnson, Marcus Peter. *One with Christ: An Evangelical Theology of Salvation*. Wheaton, IL: Crossway, 2013.

Keller, Timothy. "A Theology of Cities." Cru.org, www.cru.org /us/en/train-and-grow/leadership-training/sending-your -team/a-theology-of-cities.html. Accessed November 9, 2020.

Lewis, C. S. *Mere Christianity*. New York: HarperCollins Publishers, 2017.

Lloyd-Jones, Sally. *The Jesus Storybook Bible: Every Story Whispers His Name*. Grand Rapids: Zonderkidz, 2017.

Luther, Martin. *Christian Liberty*. Philadelphia: Fortress Press, 1957.

Ortlund, Dane Calvin. *Gentle and Lowly: The Heart of Christ for Sinners and Sufferers*. Wheaton, IL: Crossway, 2020.

Peterson, Eugene H. *Eat This Book: A Conversation in the Art of Spiritual Reading*. Grand Rapids: William B. Eerdmans Publishing Company, 2006.

———. *Long Obedience in the Same Direction*. Downers Grove, IL: InterVarsity Press, 2000.

Platt, David. *Radical: Taking Back Your Faith from the American Dream*. Colorado Springs: Multnomah Books, 2010.

Reeves, Michael. *Delighting in the Trinity: An Introduction to the Christian Faith*. Downers Grove, IL: IVP Academic, 2012.

Saint Cyprian, "The Unity of the Church." *Treatises (The Fathers of the Church, Volume 36)*, trans. Roy J. Deferrari. Washington, DC: Catholic University of America Press, 2010.

Sanders, Fred. *The Deep Things of God: How the Trinity Changes Everything* (Second Edition). Wheaton, IL: Crossway, 2017.

Smethurst, Matt. *Before You Open Your Bible: Nine Heart Postures for Approaching God's Word*. Leyland, England: 10 Publishing, 2019.

Storms, Sam. "The Love of God." *The Gospel Coalition*, www.the gospelcoalition.org/essay/the-love-of-god/.

Tozer, A. W. *Knowledge of the Holy*. New York: HarperCollins, 1961.

Treat, Jeremy R. *Seek First: How the Kingdom of God Changes Everything*. Grand Rapids: Zondervan, 2019.

Webster, John. *Holy Scripture: A Dogmatic Sketch* (Current Issues in Theology; vol. 1). Cambridge University Press, 2003.

Wilbourne, Rankin. *Union with Christ: The Way to Know and Enjoy God.* Colorado Springs: David C. Cook, 2018.

Wilkin, Jen. *None Like Him: 10 Ways God Is Different from Us (and Why That's a Good Thing).* Wheaton, IL: Crossway, 2016.

————. *In His Image: 10 Ways God Calls Us to Reflect His Character.* Wheaton, IL: Crossway, 2018.

Wright, N. T. *Simply Christian: Why Christianity Makes Sense.* New York: HarperCollins, 2010.

Wright, Tom. "Ask NT Wright Anything: #39 Will Animals Go to Heaven? . . . And Other Questions on New Creation on Apple Podcasts." *Apple Podcasts*, 30 June 2020, podcasts. apple.com/gb/podcast/39-will-animals-go-to-heaven-other-questions-on-new/id1441656192?i=1000480416847. Accessed November 9, 2020.

Also Available from
AMY GANNETT

Available where books are sold
Feb 15, 2022